ELLIOTT CARTER

AMERICAN

Composers

A list of books in the series appears at the end of this book.

Elliott Carter

James Wierzbicki

UNIVERSITY OF ILLINOIS PRESS
Urbana, Chicago, and Springfield

Manufactured in the
United States of America
1 2 3 4 5 C P 5 4 3 2 1
∞ This book is printed
on acid-free paper.

Library of Congress Cataloging-in-Publication Data
Wierzbicki, James Eugene.
Elliott Carter / James Wierzbicki.
p. cm. — (American composers)
Includes bibliographical references and index.
ISBN-13: 978-0-252-03609-5 (hardcover : alk. paper)
ISBN-10: 0-252-03609-3 (hardcover : alk. paper)
ISBN-13: 978-0-252-07800-2 (pbk. : alk. paper)
ISBN-10: 0-252-07800-4 (pbk. : alk. paper)
1. Carter, Elliott, 1908–
2. Composers—United States—Biography.
I. Title.
ML410.C3293W54 2011
780.92—dc22 2010040228
[B]

Le temps dont nous disposons chaque jour est élastique; les passions que nous ressentons le dilatent, celles que nous inspirons le rétrécissent et l'habitude le remplit.

[The time which we have at our disposal every day is elastic; the passions that we feel expand it, those that we inspire contract it; and habit fills up what remains.]

—Marcel Proust, *À l'ombre des jeunes filles en fleurs* (1919), translated by C. K. Scott Moncrieff

CONTENTS

ELLIOTT CARTER

Introduction

FOR ANY MUSICALLY TRAINED PERSON who has grappled with the intricacies of a Carter score, surely the temptation is great to focus largely on technical matters. After all, Carter's music demands extraordinary attention and precision of its performers, and for at least six decades it has been replete with "learned devices" (all-interval tetrachords, architectonic polyrhythms, metric modulations, etc.) of the sort that whet the appetites of academically inclined commentators. Whereas music of any sort is fundamentally abstract, Carter's devices seem appealingly concrete, capable not just of being identified in the "texts" of the scores but also of being rigorously analyzed and more or less easily demonstrated. The devices are in and of themselves intriguing, and they have generated a raft of commentary that purports to unravel their complexities.

Elliott Carter's music *is* complex. But it has never been music *about* complexity. In a 1976 essay titled "Music and the Time Screen," Carter reminded us that pitch and rhythmic structures form merely "the outer shell, the wrapping of the music. The reason for writing [the music]—for developing it in the way described, for weighing every note, chord, rhythm in the light of their expressive intention and their living, spontaneous interrelationships, and the judging of it all, almost unconsciously, against a private standard of what gives me genuine sensuous pleasure, of what seems fascinating, interesting, imaginative, moving, and of urgent importance—cannot be put into words."[1] Carter was right to dismiss his famous technical apparatuses as the mere "outer shell" of his music, for at least since the 1945–46 Piano Sonata the essence of his work—what makes it truly imaginative and moving—has surely been something more profound than the likes of metric modulation.

The impact of a typical Carter composition derives in part from the solidity of the work's large-scale structure and the dynamism of its small-scale fluctuations of tension and resolution. But the impact that likely strikes listeners as most immediate results from the shape and movement of the composition's various phrases. No matter how intellectually controlled are their content and design, and regardless of how well they might fit into a composition's overall plan, the individual musical statements come across as gestures that seem to spring not so much from Carter's brain as from his spirit. They declare themselves openly and eloquently; they clash with and complement one another, and they ebb and flow as forcefully as do the tides of raw feeling.

If the dynamic qualities of these gestures are analogous to human emotional states, the emotions they convey—except in those relatively few compositions that involve settings of poetry—are not at all specific. Indeed, it is precisely their ambiguity that lends Carter's gestures their potency. The amount of graspable "information" they contain is great, especially for the first-time listener. But even the first-time listener, so long as he or she remains attentive, likely senses that the received information has multiple "meanings," many of which promise to remain forever elusive. The better one knows a work by Carter, the more one realizes how much in it there is yet to be discovered. Familiarity with the music perhaps makes certain of Carter's compositional techniques seem all the more patent; at the same time, familiarity makes the real substance of Carter's music seem all the more ineffable.

Carter has often and eloquently expressed opinions about music in general and about the music of his contemporaries.[2] It is interesting, if not altogether surprising, that most of what Carter has to say about his own work in fact deals with technical matters. One of the few paragraphs in which he explains not the mechanics but the "meaning" of his music is found in his liner note for the Nonesuch recording of his 1948 Sonata for Cello and Piano. But even here one is reminded that creative persons are typically reluctant to probe too deeply into their own psyches. Although Carter is candid enough, his statement is less an independent declaration than a simple response to the observations of another writer. In his 1964 book *Music in a New Found Land*, British critic Wilfrid Mellers prefaced his chapter on Carter with these lines from Wallace Stevens's poem "Esthétique du Mal":

> And out of what one sees and hears and out
> Of what one feels, who could have thought to make
> So many selves, so many sensuous worlds,
> As if the air, the mid-day air, was swarming
> With the metaphysical changes that occur,
> Merely in living as and where we live.

Carter writes that in choosing this quotation "Mellers draws attention to some of the main aims of my work. It is quite true that I have been concerned with contrasts of many kinds of musical characters—'many selves'; with forming these into poetically evocative combinations—'many sensuous worlds'; with filling musical time and space by a web of continually varying cross references—'the air . . . swarming with . . . changes.' And to me, at least, my music grows 'Out of what one sees and hears and out / Of what one feels,' out of what occurs 'Merely . . . as and where we live.'"[3]

The 1948 Cello Sonata was the last work in which Carter maintained allegiance—but only in the second movement—to the traditional tonal system. It was also the first work in which he seriously explored, on his own terms, the idea of simultaneous and contrasting musical events that apparently had been in the back of his mind ever since his boyhood association with the American maverick composer Charles Ives.

In the 1983 first edition of his *Music of Elliott Carter*, David Schiff uses kinetic words to describe certain situations in the Cello Sonata: in the first movement the piano "marches" while the cello "swims," and even when they are moving at the same speed they seem to "collide and then bounce away from each other." In the finale, when "echoes of the second and third movements" begin to be heard, their "backward pull" is first "resisted" but then yielded to until the music finally "takes flight" and then "seems to sweep over a great peak."[4] Schiff's language is colorful but hardly fanciful. Indeed, such language sheds revealing light on the music's considerable affective power.

It was with the 1948 Cello Sonata that Carter first hit upon the mode of musical expression that best suited his message. Since then he has constantly developed this mode yet consistently held to its essence, even in such deliberately lyrical pieces as *A Mirror on Which to Dwell* (1975), *Of Challenge and of Love* (1994), and *In the Distances of Sleep* (2006). Opposition of forces is obvious just from the titles of many of Carter's instrumental works—the 1961 Double Concerto for Piano,

Harpsichord, and Two Chamber Orchestras, for example, or the 1976 Symphony of Three Orchestras, or the 1982 Triple Duo. But it figures just as importantly in his string quartets and other compositions for homogeneous ensembles. In almost all these pieces, the building blocks are compact and discrete units of musical thought—sometimes presented in isolation, as often as not superimposed or juxtaposed—whose collective impact is almost physically palpable. When a Carter pattern in a steady tempo is set against another that systematically speeds up or slows down, the listener not only observes the friction but *feels* it.

The notes that make up Carter's compositions are, after all, just notes. The notes are combined in countless intriguing ways, but to focus solely on their pitch relationships or their rhythmic patterns is to widely miss the point. Rigorously constructed though it is, Carter's work is also—in a word—stirring. Notwithstanding its abundant technical cleverness, it is its ever-present combination of "appeal" as much visceral as intellectual that allows Carter's music to rank among the twentieth century's greatest.

Of this book's four chapters, the longest is the first, which describes the circuitous path by which Carter came to arrive in the mid-1940s at his characteristic way of making music. The second chapter, dealing with the three seminal works through which Carter developed his trademark style, covers only a six-year span of Carter's very long career. In contrast, each of the third and fourth chapters focuses on a thirty-year period, the one resulting in a relatively small number of universally acknowledged masterpieces, the other resulting in a huge outpouring of mostly smaller works that posterity has yet to assess.

This is a short book and quite deliberately a nontechnical one. Readers will discover that over the book's course there is far more in-depth discussion of Carter's thinking—its philosophical underpinnings, its logic, its roots and ramifications—than of the many and diverse compositions that have resulted from it. The reason for this, I hope, will be clear enough.

Instead of writing music for complexity's sake, Elliott Carter for decades has produced complex music that deals with human experience in general and with the nature of human experience filtered through the perception of time. Apropos of this, *Elliott Carter* has as its theme the composer's time-related thoughts. If Carter's music is to be not just felt but understood, its bearing on time is surely the key.

I Foundations (1908–45)

AN UNFORTUNATELY ENDURING MYTH has it that Elliott Carter was born with the proverbial silver spoon in his mouth and that this good fortune somehow related both to Carter's intellectual grounding and to his work as a composer. Often echoed and paraphrased, the misleading idea likely stems from 1957, when Richard Franko Goldman—in one of the earliest biographical-critical studies of Carter—wrote that "as the son of a well-to-do New York family, [Carter] was not faced with the economic necessity of choosing a career, and was able to pursue an education in the leisurely fashion no longer common."[1]

It is true that Elliott Cook Carter Sr., sustaining a business launched by his father (Eli C. Carter) shortly after the American Civil War, in the early decades of the twentieth century was a successful New York–based importer of French and Belgian lace. It is not at all true, however, that Elliott Cook Carter Jr.—the composer—lived his creative life in the lap of luxury. The firm of E. C. Carter & Son was one that Elliott Carter Sr. had to *buy* from his father at a considerable price, the loans for which Carter Sr. was still repaying when his son (his only child) was born on 11 December 1908. The firm prospered only until the mid-1920s, when the American market for handmade lace curtains in essence dried up; after that, the composer's father shifted the focus of the business in turn, and always with a struggle, to knitted draperies and such relatively déclassé items as inexpensive perfumes and breath fresheners.

That Carter Jr. expressed little interest in devoting his adult life to peddling drugstore commodities caused his entrepreneurial father no end of chagrin. Carter Sr., in fact, was openly contemptuous of his son's commitment to such an impractical field as music, and in the late 1930s, when compositions by Carter Jr. began to get hearings in the New York area, Carter Sr. set a policy of not attending performances. More to the point, the always hardworking Carter Sr. *never* gifted his musically minded son with anything more than a modicum of independent income. The family's relatively secure financial status in the twentieth century's early decades indeed afforded Carter Jr. with what might be called a "good" education, first at the Horace Mann School in New York and then—from 1926 to 1932—at Harvard University. Carter's living expenses while at Harvard were of course paid for by his family, but after Harvard the young composer, in terms of finances, was pretty much on his own.

When Carter set off for Paris in 1932 primarily for the sake of studying with Nadia Boulanger, his family granted him an allowance too small for anyone to live on. Upon his return to the United States in 1935, Carter discovered that in the severely depressed economy teaching positions were almost impossible to find, and so he felt himself lucky to be able to cobble together a small income by writing reviews for the journal *Modern Music* and serving as music director for a dance company—Ballet Caravan—run by his Harvard classmate Lincoln Kirstein. He felt even more lucky to be offered—in 1940, a year after his marriage to sculptor/art critic Helen Frost-Jones—a full-time teaching position at St. John's College in Annapolis, Maryland.

Carter taught at St. John's College for only two years, his stated reason for leaving being a desire to devote himself more fully to composition. He continued to write for *Modern Music* until the summer of 1946, at which time he embarked upon his second academic appointment, at the Peabody Conservatory in Baltimore. Following his resignation from St. John's College in 1942, Carter eagerly applied for paid positions with the war-embroiled U.S. government.

His efforts to find meaningful employment (i.e., employment not just remunerative but arguably patriotic) as a translator or cryptologist all came to naught. Early in 1943, however, Carter was offered a modestly paid position as musical advisor for the New York office of the government's Office of War Information. However little it paid, this was a job that Carter took quite seriously. But it was not so time- or emotion-consuming a job that it prevented Carter from focusing on his own music. Significantly, the government work did not keep Carter from thinking long and hard about the complex machinations by which the creation of sophisticated music—or even self-consciously "difficult" music—might somehow be converted, on the eve of the twentieth century's midpoint, into a source of income. Unlike his childhood mentor, Charles Ives, Carter was never a musical amateur.

New York (1908–26)

Carter first met Ives in 1924, when he was in his fourth year at the Horace Mann School. The introduction came by way of Clifton J. Furness, the teacher at Mann assigned to guiding the students through a regimen of courses in music appreciation. Asked by interviewer Allen Edwards if at the Mann School music had been taught "as a serious thing," Carter answered that music at Mann was taken very seriously, but he added that the official curriculum focused entirely on "older music," that is, on canonic masterworks from Bach through Wagner, a repertoire that Carter said during his adolescence "bored me completely."[2]

At the Mann School, Furness dutifully taught classes in the standard repertoire, but he had a keen extracurricular interest in music of a much more daring sort. He eagerly shared this interest with Carter and like-minded Mann students (including John Bitter, son of sculptor Karl Bitter; Eugene O'Neill Jr., son of the well-known playwright; and Ivan Narodny, whose father ran a Soviet-oriented theater/art gallery in Greenwich Village). With Furness as their leader, Carter and his classmates celebrated modern music as "sort of an 'underground' affair"; before long, Carter had grown so enamored with modern music in general—so "struck by its intensity and its power," he recalled—that he committed himself to the idea that someday he would "become" a composer.[3]

Furness showed some of Ives's piano music to Carter, who had been taking lessons since the third or fourth grade and who by this time had developed both a good reading ability and a considerable amount of keyboard technique. Furness invited Carter to accompany him to private recitals given by Katherine Ruth Heyman, an English-born pianist—and self-proclaimed mystic—who championed music not just by Ives but also by such composers as Claude Debussy, Maurice Ravel, Alexander Scriabin, Arnold Schoenberg, Cyril Scott, Emerson Whithorne, Charles Tomlinson Griffes, and Dane Rudhyar. It was during the conversations that followed Heyman's recitals, which she called "séances," that the young Carter first learned of theosophy and of the American variant, launched in 1912 by

Austrian immigrant Rudolf Steiner, called anthroposophy. It was during these conversations, too, that Carter discovered that whereas Schoenberg's new serial music in the minds of at least some New York intellectuals was considered to be something of a dangerous "black art," Ives's apparently "mystical, transcendental" music had granted the composer the status of a much-reverenced "white god."[4]

"The mystical bias in all this appealed to an adolescent," Carter recalled, and so it must have been a momentous occasion when Furness, late in 1924, actually introduced Carter to Ives.[5] More than a half century after the fact, Carter fondly remembered the "dark, rainy Sunday" on which he and Furness went to Ives's residence near Gramercy Park and "stepped into a cheery, old-fashioned interior" and then "excitedly discussed modern music all afternoon."[6] The discussion must have gone well; intrigued by the teenager's wits, Ives made a habit of inviting Carter to join him and his wife in their Carnegie Hall box for New York performances by the Boston Symphony Orchestra, which under the leadership of Serge Koussevitzky was at the time (and for decades to come) the United States' premiere medium for adventurous concert-hall music.

Carter recalled that during the 1924–25 and 1925–26 seasons he met with Ives only "occasionally," most often at Carnegie Hall but sometimes at Heyman's loft or at Ives's residence.[7] Their relationship was not just cordial but sustained: the correspondence between Carter and Ives and/or his wife extends through 1954, when Ives passed away. At least in its early years, however, it was never anything more than a respectful relationship between a precocious high-school student and an arguably curmudgeonly man in his fifties who by this time had long earned his living not through musical endeavors but through management of a successful life insurance company. In the letter of recommendation requested of him when in 1926 Carter applied for admission to Harvard, Ives wrote: "Carter strikes me as rather an exceptional boy. He has an instinctive interest in literature, and especially music, that is somewhat unusual. He writes well—an essay in his school paper, 'Symbolism in Art,' shows an interesting mind. I don't know him intimately, but his teacher in Horace Mann School, Mr. Clifton J. Furness, and a friend of mine, always speaks well of him."[8]

Ives's comment that he did not know Carter "intimately" is worthy of note, and the comment seems all the more credible after careful scrutiny of Carter's various writings on Ives. Deeply appreciative as these writings are, they contain little information as to what Ives might have said, specifically, about any of the doubtless thought-provoking compositions that he heard in Carter's company. Carter's "lively talks" with Ives, it seems, tended to be of a general nature. Carter recalled:

Often [Ives] would poke fun, sit down at the piano to play from memory bits of a piece just heard, like *Daphnis et Chloé* or *Le Sacre,* taking off the Ravel major seventh chords and obvious rhythms, of the primitive repeated dissonances of Stravinsky, and calling them "too easy." "Anybody can do that," he would exclaim, playing "My Country 'Tis of Thee," the right hand in one key and the left in another. His main love, however, was for Bach, Brahms, and Franck, for he found in them spiritual elevation and nobility, which, like many a critic of his generation, he felt contemporary music had simplified away.[9]

Carter of course learned much from his conversations with Ives, but the lessons had little to do with compositional technique. For Carter, Ives was not so much a teacher as a stimulus, a role model, and—importantly—a granter of verification for Carter's status as a young intellectual.

Not surprisingly, Carter noted that it was *before* his watershed decision to be a composer that Ives's influence on him was greatest. Once Carter made the commitment, he was swept over by a desire "to learn how to write music step by step, not only by traditional methods but also from the new music that was within my grasp to imagine auditively and to formulate clear ideas about." Carter would remain deeply fond of Ives and his music, but from this point on he was driven in large part by an affinity for "clarity and sharp definition of musical material," and thus he felt "a mounting sense of frustration" whenever he returned to Ives's work because in general it "seemed so disordered and even disorganized that . . . it was nearly impossible to understand how or why much of it was put together as it was."[10]

In the summer of 1925 the sixteen-year-old Carter accompanied his father on a business trip to Vienna, in the process acquiring all the currently available scores of Arnold Schoenberg and his pupils Alban Berg and Anton Webern. In the mid-1920s, Carter recalled, music by these three Vienna-based composers was still not much heard in New York; he purchased the scores and began to study them, he said, mostly because their importance had been noted by the critic Paul Rosenfeld.[11] How much of this music Carter at the time actually understood remains unclear, even to Carter. But Carter seemed to know instinctively that the order and organization of this music—serial or otherwise—was at least *capable* of being understood and that in this respect it stood in marked contrast to the music of Ives.

Carter brought that same attitude—that is, the sure confidence that certain phenomena perhaps not immediately grasped might nevertheless indeed be built of graspable elements—to the various forms of non-Western music he explored during his high-school years. Tantalized as any teenager might be by exotic sounds but also motivated by an urgent need for syntactical understanding of "foreign" music, Carter earnestly dabbled in music from the Indonesian island of Bali (through field recordings by pioneering ethnomusicologist Colin McPhee), from China (by means of attendance not just at routine theatrical offerings in New York's Chinatown but also at New York performances by the Beijing-based Mei Lan-fang Opera Company), and from East India (via concerts featuring vocalist Ratan Devi, introduced to Carter by his high-school friend John Bitter).

Likely Carter brought that attitude as well to the sundry nonmusical works of art that during the mid-1920s caught his teenaged fancy. Perhaps owing at least in part to his friendship with schoolmate Ivan Narodny, these included numerous Soviet products of recent vintage: poetry by Vladimir Mayakovsky, for example, primitivist paintings by Nikolai Roerich, abstract paintings by Kasimir Malevitch and El Lissitsky, films directed by the likes of Alexander Pudovkin and Sergei Eisenstein. They included, too, "experiments in what now is called mixed media," Carter recalled, perhaps most notably a staged reading of Walt Whitman's *Salut au monde* "with a background of wondrous colored, moving shapes" generated by the light-projecting device called the Clavilux.[12] And they included a large amount of cutting-edge English-language literature, not the least of which were James Joyce's highly controversial 1920 novel *Ulysses* and his 1905 *Chamber Music* poems, some of which the young Carter—still just testing the waters of life as a composer—set to music and shared, to apparently encouraging response, with Ives.

Most important, Carter brought his receptive yet precociously critical attitude to the many examples of "modern" music whose performances he so hungrily sought. According to Carter's various reminiscences, the most memorable of these were pieces by Bartók, Ruggles, Schoenberg, Scriabin, Stravinsky, Varèse, and Webern. The venues ranged from downtown lofts to Carnegie Hall, and the presenters included the Franco-American Music Society, the International Composers' Guild, the League of Composers, the Philadelphia Orchestra under the direction of Leopold Stokowski, and the Boston Symphony Orchestra under the direction of Serge Koussevitzky. The deepest impressions, it seems, were made by Koussevitzky.

Asked by Edwards in 1971 if there had been "any specific instance" that set him on the path toward composition as a career, Carter—trying to focus on a single life-changing moment from almost a half century earlier—conjured up only an amalgam of memories that mixed potent first exposures to Ives's *Concord Sonata*, Varèse's *Intégrales* and *Octandre*, various orchestral and piano compositions by Scriabin, and Stravinsky's *Le sacre du printemps*. There is no telling—for Carter or for anyone else—what it was, exactly, that prompted Carter's decision to "become" a composer. But surely it was solid knowledge of Koussevitzky's adventurous programming with the BSO and Carter's perhaps naive assumptions about "all the advanced musical activity" taking place in Boston amidst Koussevitzky's glow that prompted Carter to pursue his secondary education at Harvard.[13]

Harvard (1926–32)

Located in the Boston suburb of Cambridge, Harvard indeed offered its students close proximity to Koussevitzky's orchestra and many other cultural attractions. But Koussevitzky's forward-looking agenda, as Carter saw it, was not much echoed in the syllabi of Harvard's music department. Carter matriculated into the department in the fall of 1926; he lasted only one semester, happily remaining at Harvard but opting to spend the rest of his undergraduate years in pursuit of a degree not in music but in English literature.

According to the 1971 book-length interview with Edwards, Carter's rather enormous dissatisfaction with the Harvard music department had to do primarily with the faculty's conservative attitudes. "I began to have annoying experiences of enrolling in music courses only to discover," Carter famously said, "that the professors involved couldn't stand one single thing about contemporary music and considered Koussevitzky's modernist activity at the Boston Symphony an outright scandal."[14] But an article that Carter wrote in 1946 suggests that the department twenty years earlier might not have been the bastion of conservatism that Carter later made it out to be. And more recent interviews suggest that the friction between Carter and his professors resulted from a problem much more fundamental than conflicting musical tastes.

It should be remembered that up to this time Carter—aside from his piano lessons and his classes in music appreciation at the Horace Mann School and despite his close relationship with Charles Ives—had had absolutely no formal instruction in music composition or in any of the analytical methods that nowadays (albeit mostly in the United States) are grouped under the rubric of "music theory." It seems that simply by listening Carter had acquired knowledge aplenty about the expressive essence of the various modernist pieces that so powerfully caught his adolescent attention. But Carter very much wanted to learn how these pieces, in a technical sense, "worked." "I would have been glad if somebody at Harvard had explained to me what went on in the music of Stravinsky, Bartók, and Schoenberg," Carter told Edwards, "and had tried somehow to develop in me the sense of harmony and counterpoint that these composers had."[15] But explanations of this sort, Carter said, were not to be found in any of Harvard's music classes. Nor was there to be found, Carter soon discovered, basic instruction in the rudiments of music.

In 1946 Carter penned an article that celebrated the career to date of Walter Piston, who joined the Harvard faculty in 1926 and with whom Carter studied composition for the sake of an MA degree in 1930–32. Contradicting his own later comments on the music department's overall stodginess, Carter noted that during Piston's undergraduate years at Harvard (1920–24) "the placid routine of college music teaching began to be disturbed by the strangeness of the new music. Few had the vision of [Edward Burlingame] Hill, who kept his annual course in modern French music up to date with the latest scores from Paris." He also noted that one of Piston's fellow undergraduates, Virgil Thomson, organized a performance of Erik Satie's 1918 protominimalist cantata *Socrate* that "is still talked about" and that composition students regularly brought in works that "seemed to flout every idea that teachers believed in."[16]

Piston earned his bachelor's degree in 1924 and then studied for two years in Paris. Upon his return in 1926—the same year in which Carter began his undergraduate education—he joined the Harvard faculty as a full-time lecturer. Even before he left for Paris, Carter wrote, Piston "was completely won over to new music and, following all the performances of recent works, studying scores, he was able to master many of its techniques." One of the compositions that Piston brought back with him from Paris was his Three Pieces for Flute, Clarinet, and Bassoon, something that, Carter noted, "impressed many forward-looking musicians at once." Significantly, Carter pointed out that not just Piston but other members of the Harvard music faculty circa 1926, in response as much to trends in contemporary music as to recent research in historical musicology, were participating in "a complete revision of courses in music theory." Carter recalled that Piston, who taught classes in harmony and counterpoint, was especially responsive to the challenge of updating the curriculum. "As a progressive new theory teacher," Carter wrote, "Piston tackled this problem and went to its core, attacking it in much the same analytic way that he applied to the study of contemporary scores."[17]

Clearly, the Harvard music department in 1926 was not just a place—as Carter often later implied, always with a colorful tone of sarcasm—for people "destined to be church organists."[18] With Hill and Piston on the faculty, the curriculum indeed included serious discussion of contemporary music. At the same time, however, the curriculum assumed on the part of first-year students a fair amount of competency in counterpoint and traditional harmony; it was expected, in other words, that freshmen concentrating in music already knew how to harmonize a melody in the four-part chorale style of Bach, or how to realize an eighteenth-century figured bass, or how to compose short pieces of their own in the manner of, say, Mendelssohn or Brahms.

Carter recently told an interviewer that during his first semester at Harvard he took "a rather solid harmony course with Walter Spalding," at the time the music department's head. Given an assignment to harmonize a tune, Carter responded with an atonal treatment in the manner of Schoenberg. "When they saw that," Carter said, "everybody laughed so much that I decided English literature would be a little safer."[19]

This is a telling comment, and it counters the much-repeated idea—likely stemming from the interview with Edwards—that Carter abandoned Harvard's music department out of frustration with its old-fashioned tastes and methods. The eighteen-year-old Carter might well have been frustrated with the Harvard faculty's apparent dismissal of his modernist musical heroes. But a more potent source of frustration—and probably of embarrassment—was the fact that the department's rigorous demands were simply over Carter's head.

Carter seems to have experienced at least two significant epiphanies during his first semester at Harvard. One of them, described above, involved his quick and more or less public recognition that the Harvard music department, for reasons as much technical as aesthetic, was not an environment in which his ebullient yet untrained creative spirit was likely to thrive. The other was his private realization that the compositions he had written over the previous several years—compositions in the manner, variously, of Ives, or Schoenberg, or Varèse—were really not very good.

As an energetic high-school student, Carter earnestly tried to produce music that emulated the styles of all his most revered models. But by the time he matriculated to Harvard, he told an interviewer in 2002, he had become aware that with his limited skills he "could never write anything that [he] liked or [that seemed] worthwhile." Apparently entering adulthood at the same time he entered college, Carter literally threw out all those early efforts, knowing that hitherto his adolescent "tastes [had been] far more advanced than [his] abilities" and that if he truly intended to be a composer it was necessary for him, indeed, "to make a serious study."[20]

At least for Carter, serious study of the more basic elements of so-called music theory was not to be had at Harvard. So Carter looked elsewhere for the practical training he knew he needed; he found it at the Longy School of Music, an independent conservatory that had been established in 1915 by BSO oboist Georges Longy and that ten years later, under the directorship first of Longy's daughter and then of Minna Holl, had begun a period of substantial growth. In 1927, when Carter withdrew from Harvard's music program, the Longy School was still based in Longy's home, a large house just two blocks from Symphony Hall in Boston; conveniently for Carter, in 1930 the school relocated to Cambridge.

Curiously, the Longy School is mentioned not at all in any of the three books—the 1971 extended interview with Edwards, the massive 1977 volume titled *The Writings of Elliott Carter*, the 1997 anthology of essays and lectures edited by Jonathan W. Bernard—that together contain most, if not all, of the "official" statements that Carter has made about his life and work. An early biographical account of Carter, in David Ewen's 1949 dictionary-like *American Composers Today*, mentions that at the Longy School Carter studied solfège with Hans Ebell and took piano lessons with Newton Swift; both the 1983 first edition and the 1998 second edition of David Schiff's *The Music of Elliott Carter* note that Carter during his Harvard years studied not just music theory but also oboe at the Longy School; but only in the very recently published *Elliott Carter: A Centennial Portrait in Letters and Documents* is Carter's oboe teacher—Louis Speyer, at the time the English horn player with the BSO—actually named.[21] While other writers on Carter have opted to dance lightly around the matter of Carter's studies at Longy, the authors of the just-mentioned book boldly state—apparently with Carter's approval—that "the bulk of [Carter's] musical training took place initially at the Longy School of Music."[22]

To date, musico-historical writing on Carter's collegiate years has focused on the composer's not very productive involvement with the famous music department at Harvard. There is a crying need, it would seem, for deep and thorough examination of Carter's apparently quite fruitful involvement with the not-so-famous Longy School. Scholars attracted to this potentially rich vein of inquiry might consider the fact that Nadia Boulanger, the internationally renowned French pedagogue with whom Carter sought tutelage immediately after his Harvard stint, chose Longy for her base of operations (from 1938 to 1944) after the climate in Europe took a drastic turn for the worse. Scholars wondering just how much Carter learned at Longy might also consider a letter to the editor that Carter submitted to the *Journal of Music Theory* in 1963, three years after he had won the first of his two Pulitzer Prizes (for his 1959 String Quartet No. 2) and almost two decades after the earliest manifestations of what, in the 1960s and later, would be commonly regarded as "the Carter style." The letter expresses Carter's desire that there be a standardization of notation for complex rhythms of the sort that by this time characterized his own compositions, and for a model it offers the notational system that Carter himself used and that was based on a scheme first proposed in the 1925 *Principles of Musical Theory* by Renée Longy-Miquelle.[23]

Speaking only for himself, not for other members of the 1926 freshman cohort, Carter recently told an interviewer: "The Harvard music department always had a fundamental problem, and that is, you get these students who are so intelligent, so cultivated, who know about music, but they have no musical training. That's why I went to study at the Longy School, because I didn't have ear training; and I learned a lot there, that I never would have learned at Harvard."[24] Indeed. On the other hand, it seems that Carter at Harvard—once emancipated from what he perceived to be a restrictive music department—learned quite "a lot" that likely he would never have learned had he followed the conservatory-based instructional path that by the mid-1920s had become the norm for would-be American composers.

Carter switched, after his first semester at Harvard, from the music department to the program in English literature. For his required secondary areas of concentration he opted for classics and philosophy, and for electives he chose courses in German and mathematics.

The 1957 statement by Richard Franko Goldman quoted early in this chapter—to the effect that Carter, being born into supposedly well-to-do circumstances, was "leisurely" able to pursue an education without concern for how that education might enable him to earn a living—is for the most part egregiously off the mark. Goldman should have known that collegiate deans of admission in the 1920s—as surely they did at the time of Goldman's writing, and as surely they still do today—would have counseled parents of prospective students that a bachelor's degree in *any* of the so-called liberal arts was hardly akin to a trade-school certificate. The only thing even remotely correct in Goldman's statement is the suggestion that a liberal-arts education of the sort that Carter received at Harvard is, among composers, "no longer common."

Whereas Goldman mistakenly focused on the impracticality of Carter's studies at Harvard, Jonathan W. Bernard more accurately has concentrated on the overall richness of Carter's undergraduate education. In almost all his classes, Bernard writes, "Carter was exposed to a certain kind of intellectual training that is rarely encountered in a composer's education." Bernard argues effectively that almost all of Carter's mature music has to do in one way or another with the nature of time. Considering that this mature music did not begin to appear until the composer was almost forty years old, Bernard seems to state the obvious when he notes that "Carter's insight into the true role of time in music had a long gestation." But then he makes the point—a sharp and telling point, and one missed by many writers who have dealt with Carter in dictionary entries and liner notes for recordings—that the origins of this insight "owed more to [Carter's] general humanist education than to his specifically musical training."[25]

Carter's "general humanist education"—his study of what it means to be genuinely "human"—began with his studies at the Horace Mann School. During Carter's high-school days this education was furthered, albeit in informal ways, by the several visits to Europe that Carter made in the company of his father and by the many excursions that Carter excitedly undertook, usually with like-minded friends of various ages, into various regions of New York's avant-garde arts world.

As a high-school student, Carter enjoyed the unbridled luxury of being an omnivorous consumer of intellectual-artistic stimuli. As a Harvard undergraduate, Carter was reined in, and doubtless this was to his benefit. There was no stopping Carter's appetite for new material, especially material somehow modernist in style and content. At the same time, Carter at Harvard was taught a disciplined approach to material old as well as new. Carter was rigorously trained, in other words, in modes of critical thinking.

His base of operations at Harvard was the English department, which in some respects had a curriculum as conservative as Carter thought the music department's to be. "The detailed study of English literature . . . in those days stopped with Tennyson," Carter told Edwards, but he happily "supplemented" the absorption of required texts by reading "William Carlos Williams, Marianne Moore, T. S. Eliot, Hopkins, Cummings, Joyce, Lawrence, Stein, and others."[26] One of Carter's strictest teachers was George Lyman Kittredge, at the time acknowledged worldwide for his still-in-progress editions of Shakespeare and famous on campus for leading undergraduates through various Shakespeare plays and the works of Chaucer at an extraordinarily slow pace. Another teacher was Irving Babbitt, often credited as being one of the founders of the field known today as comparative literature and in the 1920s best known for having launched the movement—fundamentally antiromanticist yet critical of the excesses of modernism—called the New Humanism.

Babbitt's lectures were especially influential on Carter, who entered Harvard with a modernist fire in his belly but also—one surmises, judging from the expressive essence of almost all his mature works—with an abiding romanticist spirit deep in his heart. Indeed, Carter recalled that Babbitt's thinking played "an important role" in his own reconsideration of the various manifestations of modernist art that had so excited him during his adolescence. In particular, Carter recalled, some of Babbitt's lectures—based on ideas first expressed in Babbitt's 1910 *The New Laokoön: An Essay on the Confusion of the Arts*—drove home the idea that there were "certain limits beyond which art could not go without destroying itself and becoming meaningless."[27]

Likely even more influential on Carter, pursuing a minor in philosophy, were the lectures given by Alfred North Whitehead. Whitehead had joined the Harvard faculty shortly before Carter's matriculation. His formal education and academic career up to this point, in England, had been anchored in departments of mathematics; before the 1920s his most major claim to fame was the coauthoring, with Bertrand Russell, of the 1910–13 *Principia Mathematica.* But his interests also included physics, logic, theology, metaphysics, and—importantly—the theory of science and education. Whitehead wrote about all these topics in an elegantly Platonist manner, and this resulted in his being invited in 1924 to join the Harvard faculty as professor not of mathematics but of philosophy. In 1927, the year after Carter began his studies at Harvard, Whitehead visited the University of Edinburgh to deliver the prestigious Gifford Lectures. Two years later these lectures were published as *Process and Reality,* a text usually credited as being the foundation for the still current theistic-metaphysical movement known as process philosophy.

Vis-à-vis Carter and the rhythmically complex music he would begin to compose some two decades after his Harvard experience, the most impressive element of Whitehead's thinking—the idea that for Carter "made the 'modern' much more comprehensible," the idea that Carter said "molded my thinking—[and] not only about music"—seems to have been what Whitehead called the "principle of organism."[28] In the collections of his writings and lectures, the closest Carter comes to elaborating on Whitehead's principle of organism is to be found in an appreciation of composer Goffredo Petrassi penned in 1960 for a proposed but never launched Italian journal. Carter notes that in creating his richly textured recent music Petrassi in fact was thinking less in terms of textures than of events, "reminding one of the meaning of 'event' in the sense defined by Alfred North Whitehead: as a unit of action in a total sequence in which the event contains within itself not only its own history but as well its prefiguration of possible futures and its own individualized character."[29]

A pithy summary of the principle of organism—aided by a book aptly titled *Understanding Whitehead*—is offered by Bernard in his 1995 "Elliott Carter and the Modern Meaning of Time." Stemming from Albert Einstein's theories of relativity, Whitehead's principle posits an "organism" not as a quasi-biological entity but as "a temporally bound process which *organizes* a variety of given elements into a new fact."[30] For Whitehead, the "ultimate realities" of any phenomenon are not mere bits of data but the "transient experiences" of the phenomenon's observers.[31] As Bernard neatly puts it, according to Whitehead's principle of organism, "our understanding of how things work together" depends not on our "sense-perception of individual or isolated moments or elements" but, rather, on our comprehension of "the way in which [these moments or elements] 'require each other,' to use Whitehead's phrase: the causal links that they form among themselves."[32]

"If all this seems rather abstract," Bernard writes, "one must recognize that Carter had in a way been prepared to absorb such ideas before he even arrived at college, not through reading philosophy, but through exposure to some of the newest and most innovative literature of his day."[33] Bernard mentions in particular Carter's keen interest, while still a high-school student, in James Joyce's *Ulysses* and, beginning in 1927, in Marcel Proust's *Remembrance of Things Past.* But Carter as a college student was also interested in and likely inspired by the fiction of Thomas Mann and the other authors (noted above) with which he "supplemented" his required reading at Harvard. He was interested, too, in the poetry of William Carlos Williams and Robert Frost, in the films of Serge Eisenstein and Jean Renoir, in the visual art not just of the Russian avant-gardists but also of the American painters John Marin and Joseph Stella, in the philosophical ideas not just of Whitehead but also of Henri Bergson, Martin Heidegger, and Edmund Husserl.

While Carter's ingestion of all this indeed started during his high-school years, his digestion of it did not begin until Carter settled in at Harvard, and it was aided not just by his formal courses in English literature and philosophy but also, importantly, by conversations with such like-minded classmates as James Agee, Ralph Kirkpatrick, and Lincoln Kirstein. Still, it would be almost twenty years before the input fully metabolized, before it manifested itself in works representative of the singular musical style by which—notwithstanding that style's many twists and turns—Carter is known today.

After his first college semester, Carter "officially" pursued his musical studies only at the Longy School. But this is not to say that he isolated himself from music-related activities at Harvard or that he abandoned the things that drew him to Cambridge in the first place.

During his entire period at Harvard, Carter told Edwards, he attended concerts by Koussevitzky's BSO "two or three times a week" as well as concerts by the Boston Pops, whose conductor, the Italian composer Alfredo Casella, "managed to sandwich large amounts of new music in between old favorites." And early in his Cambridge years Carter made the acquaintance of Henry F. Gilbert, a composer six years older than Charles Ives who, like Ives, existed somewhat on the fringe of mainstream American musical life despite some early prestigious successes. "I used to visit [him] often at his run-down but hospitable house," Carter told Edwards, and "the easy-going bohemianism of his family and himself, with his downright American humor, was a great relief after the tensions of Harvard."[34]

Despite the personal tensions that Carter—with a modernist chip on his shoulder—must have experienced during his ill-advised first and only semester as a student in Harvard's music department, over the course of his undergraduate education, as his understanding and appreciation of older scores grew, Carter frequently availed himself of the rich holdings of the Harvard music library. Significantly, despite his initial aversion to older music, Carter as an upperclassman successfully auditioned for the Harvard Glee Club, then directed by Archibald Davison, and he also sang "as a hoarse tenor in a Bach cantata club."[35] With Clifford Furness, his teacher at the Horace Mann School, Carter participated in December 1928 as pianist in a concert of contemporary music presented at a private residence. And of course he paid close attention to but did not participate in the concerts given by the Pierian Sodality, a Harvard-based student orchestra that under the direction of Nicolas Slonimsky reveled in an "orgy of first performances" that fairly "rocked the [Harvard] Yard."[36]

Carter being always reluctant to discuss his juvenile efforts, it is difficult to know just how much music he composed or attempted to compose during his undergraduate years. One of the few pieces that has survived—only because a manuscript copy was discovered in the archives of the journal *New Music*, to which the song had been hopefully submitted—is a short setting of the James Joyce poem "My Love Is in a Light Attire." As Schiff observes, this clearly "is not the work of a compositional prodigy."[37]

Likewise not especially prodigious is the single composition that survives from the two-year period (1930–32) during which Carter, having earned his bachelor's degree in English literature, returned to Harvard's music department to pursue an MA in composition. This incidental music for a production by the Harvard Classical Club of Sophocles' play *Philoctetes* to a certain extent reflects Carter's Harvard studies in Greek with Milman Parry, his oboe lessons at the Longy School, and the time he spent—during the summer following his freshman year—in Tunisia making transcriptions for Baron Rudolphe d'Erlanger's in-progress book *La musique arabe.* In any case, it is scored for tenor and baritone soloists, men's chorus, oboe, and the North African frame drum called the darabukka; holding to the model of ancient bardic singing at the time being researched by Parry, the setting of the Greek text is entirely syllabic and accented according to prevailing rules of scansion, and the harmonic-melodic language explores in turn various Greek modes as they were then understood. An unsigned review in the *Harvard Crimson* noted that the score made "no attempt . . . to adhere pedantically to the canons of Greek music" but nevertheless skillfully managed to imitate Greek music's "general nature and effect."[38] Rather less enthusiastically, Schiff later observed, after perusing the manuscript score, that the *Philoctetes* music "gives little indication of [Carter's] talent."[39]

Directed by Parry, with the Classical Club's seven-voice chorus led by E. C. Weist, and with Louis Sperry (Carter's oboe teacher at the Longy School) and percussionist C. T. Murphy as the featured instrumentalists, *Philoctetes* received two performances in the dining hall of Harvard's Lowell House in March 1933. The music's composer was not around to witness the production or to share in the applause. By this time, after having spent two years intensively studying composition and orchestration with Walter Piston and trying to gain whatever Gustav Holst had to offer during his brief stint as a visiting professor at Harvard, Carter had settled himself in Paris.

Paris (1932–35)

Fluent in French since his early childhood and during his grade-school and high-school years having traveled often to France with his father, Carter under any circumstances likely would have chosen Paris as the base of operations for his years abroad. In his father's company, the young Carter had visited Germany and Austria as well, but his memories of those countries in the aftermath of World War I were discolored by images of "chalky, ruined fields where only a few scraggly weeds would grow" and, in the cities, "waiters [snatching] uneaten food off plates before their hungry colleagues could."[40] Although Carter in the early 1930s was still intrigued by the music of Schoenberg and his students and by German expressionist painting, his awareness of recent political events in Berlin and Munich gave him a profound distaste for most things Teutonic.

Carter had a natural predisposition for Paris. But it was largely the urgings of Walter Piston, for two years his composition teacher at Harvard, that finalized his decision not just to relocate to Paris but to partake of instruction with Nadia

Boulanger. Since 1920 Boulanger had taught classes in harmony at Paris's École normale de musique, and since 1921 she had taught as well at the American Conservatory located in the Paris suburb of Fontainebleau.[41] Upon his graduation from Harvard in 1924, Piston was awarded the music department's John Knowles Paine Traveling Fellowship, and he used it for a two-year residency in Paris during which he worked not just with Boulanger but also with Paul Dukas; upon his return to Harvard in 1926, Piston repeatedly sang the praises, in particular, of Boulanger. Despite being told by Charles Ives that a genuinely "red-blooded American" composer should remain on his native soil, Carter took Piston's advice and—following a path trod before him not just by Piston but also by the likes of Aaron Copland, Virgil Thomson, and Roy Harris—in the late summer of 1932 began instruction with Boulanger.[42]

Likening Carter to the central character of Henry James's novel *The American*, David Schiff suggests that the twenty-two-year-old composer, "well-mannered, fluent in French, and Harvard-educated," "may have given a few signs to his new mentor of the Christopher Newman within himself."[43] But Carter, quite unlike the James protagonist, did not come to the City of Light with pocketfuls of money.

There are differing accounts as to just how impoverished Carter was during the years he spent in Paris. Felix Meyer and Anne C. Shreffler, in their recent *Centennial Portrait*, note that "Carter remembers that his mother gave him $1000 per year while he was studying in Paris."[44] They also note that Carter recalled—as has been reported in other biographical and autobiographical summaries—that when Boulanger heard of this seemingly generous subsidy she demanded fully half of it for her annual instructional fee, but she relented when she learned from other students that Carter in fact was struggling to support himself by doing such odd jobs as copying music, teaching English, and singing in a church choir.[45] On the other hand, Schiff, in the 1983 first edition of his *Music of Elliott Carter*, wrote that Carter's father, apparently incensed over his son's decision to spend his post-Harvard years studying music, "promptly cut his allowance to five hundred dollars a year."[46] Perhaps Carter received allowances from both his father and his mother. In any case, Paris in the early 1930s was an international capital where even for students the cost of living was relatively high. For Carter, simply getting by "involved sacrifices if not squalor," and likely he was not exaggerating when he told Schiff that "his teeth never recovered from those years of neglect."[47]

Carter, of course, went to Paris neither for dental work nor—as was the case with James's fictional character—for a quick and massive dose of Continental sophistication. Nor did he go to Paris, and specifically to Boulanger, in order to learn the workings of the contemporary music that long fascinated him.

It was while he was studying with Boulanger, Carter told Edwards, that he "began for the first time to get an intellectual grasp of what went on technically in modern works."[48] Notwithstanding his recent studies with Piston, perhaps this was so. But Boulanger had little interest in either the techniques or the content of modern works; although she admired the music of Stravinsky, she generally detested, with the exception of certain pieces by Webern, the compositions of the Germans and Austrians, and the only recent music she claimed to actually enjoy—music by Francis Poulenc and Henri Sauguet, for example—was of a remarkably conservative stripe. It may be that Carter indeed began to understand modern music during his years with Boulanger, but a good case can be made, as Schiff did in 1983, that "Carter did not *need* Mlle Boulanger as an introduction to modernism."[49] Rather, Carter needed Mlle Boulanger as an instructor in something he received neither at Harvard nor at the Longy School: basic training in the craft of musical composition.

"My own ineptitude" circa 1932 "worried me deeply," Carter recalled a half century later, "and I was willing to do anything to learn how to overcome it, and to gain the kind of command I would need to write the kind of music I aspired to write."[50]

Boulanger was sympathetic to Carter's needs and respectful of his expressed humility, but the instruction she gave him was in essence not much different from what she offered her more advanced, more confident students. Some of it involved criticism of her students' compositional efforts, a large part of it involved the analytical study of music dating as far back as Machaut, and an even larger part involved exercises in harmony and counterpoint. Carter had taken classes in harmony and counterpoint during his graduate studies at Harvard, and, notwithstanding his later confession of "ineptitude," he told Edwards that upon his arrival in Paris he felt he "knew all about these subjects." "Nevertheless," he added, "when Nadia Boulanger put me back on tonic and dominant chords in half-notes, I found to my surprise that I learned all kinds of things I'd never thought of before."[51]

His lessons with Boulanger fell into three basic categories. When Carter brought in his assignments in counterpoint or, later, in canon and fugue, Boulanger would quickly point out any objective flaws and then spend time demonstrating how here or there the voice leading might have been more creatively handled or how this or that motif might have been more interestingly expanded. When Carter brought in the occasional original composition, Boulanger would read through it and then discuss whatever it was about the effort—usually some negative quality, such as overuse of a potentially "special" effect or the weakening of a new section's "character" by too many perhaps unintentional references to the previous section—that happened to catch her attention. When Carter came to a lesson empty-handed, Boulanger would simply talk to him about music in general.

"Sometimes," Carter recalled, Boulanger's talking took the form of a more or less formal "lecture about care in workmanship, pointing out that a good workman took care of details, even those that were not immediately visible." He remembered that

> [Boulanger] would turn over a chair, for instance, in the living room and show how the workmanship in that chair was not good, and that the fact that it hadn't been carefully worked on even in an invisible place somehow vitiated the effect of the chair, which if it had all been carefully worked at everywhere would have made a very much better, more beautiful and more striking impression. Or she would point out that even the most relaxed moments of Mozart or Stravinsky were not filled with *pacotille* (cheap material) but with musically imaginative, valuable touches. At another time, she would discuss some piece of music she had been thinking about, perhaps one of the Bach cantatas we had been singing, or a mass by Josquin des Près, and she would call to my attention modulations, developments of themes, or linear beauties.[52]

It is difficult to measure the relative weight, in terms of their effect on the "mature" music that Carter would begin to produce in the late 1940s, of these various kinds of lessons that Carter more than a decade earlier had had with Boulanger. Certainly Carter, by slogging for three years through increasingly demanding exercises in counterpoint under Boulanger's guidance, learned a great deal about musical craftsmanship. And certainly in Boulanger's studio he learned vis-à-vis his own recent compositional efforts to be rigorously critical, to the extent that he destroyed all of them before leaving Paris.

But even Carter remains unsure of what, precisely, he learned from Boulanger. In 1971 he told Edwards that "the things that were most remarkable and wonderful about [Boulanger] were her extreme concern for the material of music and her acute awareness of its many phases and possibilities."[53] Twenty or so years later he remarked appreciatively on Boulanger's "deep devotion to music, [her] sense of responsibility, [her] ability to pay careful attention to each note," yet he admitted that "what I actually learned from her is still somewhat undefinable."[54]

Perhaps the greatest dividend of Carter's study with Boulanger was simply a holistic attitude not just toward music per se but toward all that might be expressed through music. "The extraordinary example of personal quality that Nadia Boulanger set was really what was important," Carter wrote. "It was an impressive view of life and art, impelling one to make important demands on oneself, to pay strict attention to the material of the music and to make the very best choices one could, choices that were, one hoped, beautiful and also particularly eloquent. I have a feeling that I never would have composed the kind of music I began to produce around 1940 if I hadn't been taught this human lesson."[55]

Significantly, the "human lesson" taught day by day by Boulanger meshed in fruitful ways with the humanities-based education that Carter had acquired at Harvard. Just as significantly, Carter's diligent fulfillment of Boulanger's assignments in harmony and counterpoint left him with the genuine feeling—a feeling he had never experienced during his high-school days or at Harvard—that at long last he actually knew something about musical technique.

Assessing his own development but likely thinking only of the distinctly "Carteresque" works that did not begin to appear until the mid-1940s, Carter was doubtless right when he opined that whatever he learned from Boulanger "produced no real result until a number of years after [he] had left" Boulanger's care.[56] Yet Carter, shortly after his Paris sojourn, produced a substantial amount of music that he did not find it necessary to destroy. It seems that Carter gained from his years with Boulanger not just musical craftsmanship but also, importantly, a healthy measure of self-confidence. As Schiff has aptly observed, it was only "after Paris" that Carter "could begin to compose."[57]

Back in the United States (1935–45)

Carter began to compose, after Paris, in the same place that he had tentatively started to compose a few years earlier. His destination upon returning to the United States in May 1935 was Cambridge, Massachusetts, where the same Harvard Classical Club that had performed his incidental music for *Philoctetes* commissioned him to write comparable music for a production of Plautus's *Mostellaria.*

Whereas the *Philoctetes* score had the club's male singers accompanied only by oboe and percussion, the *Mostellaria* music featured a chamber orchestra. The scheduled production (set for April 1936) never took place, but the prologue—titled *Tarantella* and with a text not by Plautus but by Ovid (from his *Fasti*)—received a performance by the Harvard Glee Club on 5 March 1937. More significant in terms of Carter's budding career, G. Wallace Woodworth, the glee club conductor who in effect "discovered" the *Tarantella* and brought about its piano-supported premiere, two months later led a Boston Pops performance with the original chamber-orchestra accompaniment.[58]

The vocal medium suited Carter, who as a Harvard student had lent his voice to various campus ensembles and who during his years in Paris not only studied the vocal works of a great many Renaissance and early Baroque composers but also participated, in weekly sessions at Boulanger's apartment, in the singing at sight of virtually all the Bach cantatas. Perhaps inspired by the modest but nonetheless apparent success of his *Tarantella*, Carter in 1937 and 1938 produced four more choral pieces and a song that in short order had public performances. The first of these was *Let's Be Gay*, a work for women's chorus and two pianos based on texts by John Gay. It was written for and duly performed in the spring of 1938 by the Wells College Glee Club, which at the time was led by Carter's friend Nicolas Nabokov. After this came a pair of relatively simple, quasi-modal works with texts by Robert Herrick for unaccompanied mixed chorus (*Harvest Home* and *To Music*). They were envisioned as part of a never-completed large set of "modern madrigals" and appropriately premiered—in New York, also in the spring of 1938—by the Lehman Engel Madrigal Singers. On commission, early in 1938 Carter made a setting for alto voice and guitar, in the manner of an Elizabethan lute song, of "Tell Me Where Is Fancy Bred" for a radio production by Orson Welles's Mercury Theatre of Shakespeare's *The Merchant of Venice*. Also on commission, in December 1938 Carter composed—for Lazare Saminsky and his chorus at New York's prestigious Temple Emanu-El—an a cappella treatment of Emily Dickinson's poem "Heart Not So Heavy as Mine." The Dickinson setting was premiered in March 1939, and, importantly, it was the first of Carter's compositions to be published.

But Carter upon his return from Europe was involved not just with vocal music but also with instrumental music, especially with instrumental music that related to dance. Carter's various reminiscences of his time in Paris fondly allude to the considerable amount of time he spent hungrily absorbing stimuli not just musical but also visual at the ballet. Carter's reminiscences note, too, that it was in Paris that he connected from time to time with Lincoln Kirstein, who by this time had already started on the path that would take him, within just a few years, to a position of unrivaled dominance in the international community of ballet impresarios. Carter and Kirstein together had much admired the work of the young Russian choreographer George Balanchine, and while still in Paris Kirstein even dared to form a Balanchine-oriented dance troupe called Ballets 1933. Returning to the United States more or less simultaneous with Carter, Kirstein made preparations to launch a company called Ballet Caravan. The impact of the company's debut, Kirstein hoped, would result at least in part from a balletic presentation of a solidly American story that combined daring choreography with comparably bold new music. For such music, Kirstein first approached Virgil Thomson; the offer to Thomson being declined, Kirstein then turned to Carter. Well in advance of Ballet Caravan's official debut, Carter early in the summer of 1936 finished a piano sketch for the music that three years later—much expanded and in full orchestral regalia—would accompany Ballet Caravan's production of *Pocahontas.*

Shortly after completing the sketch for *Pocahontas* and being appointed musical director of Kirstein's envisioned dance company, Carter moved from Cambridge to New York. He was twenty-eight years old, doubtless filled with confidence about his recently acquired technical skills and likely satisfied more than a little with the harmonically bold, rhythmically aggressive music he had just concocted for Kirstein. But the United States in 1936 was still a long way from recovering from the economic crisis known as the Great Depression. Although a small allowance from his father helped him keep body and soul together, it would be months before Carter earned even a penny from the vocal compositions mentioned above, and academic positions, which Carter hoped might be readily available to someone with a Harvard-Boulanger pedigree, in fact were nowhere to be found. Faced with the serious task of having to earn a living, Carter—with obvious embarrassment—wrote to Piston:

> In looking for a job to carry me through the year I have swallowed my pride deciding to give a try as a music critic, so that I can have a chance to hear many concerts. Of all the evils I have thought that for the present this would, if I could get a job in this capacity, solve my financial problem and at the same time give me a certain amount of leisure to compose.
>
> I know your opinion of this work. . . . I dislike the whole idea of having to be both critical and political myself but in the present situation I do not see any other type of work.[59]

It is not known if Carter applied for positions on the music staffs of any of the many newspapers that at the time flourished—despite the depressed economy—in all the large East Coast cities and that, even to an entry-level full-time employee, would have paid a relatively good salary. All that is known is that Carter late in 1936 signed on as a regular contributor to *Modern Music*, an erudite journal founded in 1924 as a platform for the New York–based League of Composers and sustained, through 1946, by editor/publisher Minna Lederman.

Luckily for Carter, his assignments to cover performances of new music not just in New York but also in Boston, Philadelphia, and Washington, D.C., provided him not just with a bit of cash but also with easy access to the venues in which this music was presented. Luckily for posterity, the thirty-one Carter-signed pieces that appeared in *Modern Music* between early 1937 and the summer of 1946 give a fair representation of Carter's tastes and prejudices during an important stage of his development. Together, as Else and Kurt Stone note, these writings "reveal their author to be a youthful, musically sensitive and knowledgeable, well-educated, idealistic, and occasionally somewhat rash rebel in search of a more perfect musical world in which a truly American new music, free from the thrall of European influences, could flourish unhampered by a conservative American Establishment."[60]

To his credit, Carter's early articles for *Modern Music* do not reveal any of the frustration he surely felt as a young composer trying both to find his voice and, on a more practical level, to break into the competitive New York music scene. The several minor successes Carter achieved with choral music during his first years of repatriation have been noted above. But during this same period Carter also experienced what by at least one standard of measurement—that is, Carter's own critical judgment—might be considered failures. The one-page entry on Carter in Claire R. Reis's 1938 *Composers in America* tellingly lists works that had been recently completed but, for one reason or another, destroyed. Impressively, these include two string quartets, a sonata for flute and piano, a concerto for English horn and orchestra, a symphony, and a one-act opera titled *Tom and Lily*.[61]

Reis's entry on Carter of course includes the *Pocahontas* music, which at the time of Reis's writing was still very much in progress but which in its embryonic forms, with choreography by Lew Christensen, had been successfully making the rounds at dance festivals and workshops since the late summer of 1936. Sharing a triple bill with William Dollar's *Air and Variations* (accompanied by selections from Bach's *Goldberg Variations*) and Eugene Loring's *Billy the Kid* (propelled by a new score from Aaron Copland), Christensen's *Pocahontas* had its official premiere at the Martin Beck Theatre in New York on 24 May 1939. Most of the critical attention went to *Billy the Kid;* in line with most of his journalistic colleagues, the *New York Times*' dance critic, John Martin, dismissed Christensen's work as "modernistic and stuffy," and he noted that "Mr. Carter's music is so thick it is hard to see the stage through it."[62] But others in the New York community apparently had a different opinion at least of Carter's music.

Copland certainly admired it. On his recommendation Carter in the fall of 1939 sent a suite from *Pocahontas* to Koussevitzky, who apparently found the score to be quite "brilliant" but "too light for introducing your name for the first time in the Boston Symphony programs."[63] More significant for Carter, in June 1940 the *New York Times* announced that the *Pocahontas* score had won "the Juilliard School's annual competition for the publication of orchestral works by American composers."[64] And with this public affirmation, finally, Carter's career as a composer was launched.

In July 1939, shortly after the premiere of *Pocahontas*, Carter married Helen Frost-Jones, a sculptor and art critic to whom he had been introduced by Nabokov and with whom he had already been living "for quite a long time."[65] Perhaps because of his new status as a married man, Carter redoubled his efforts to find a real job. As he had done when he first returned from Europe, he again explored the academic job market, and he found that this time around—with not just public performances of his music but also several awards to his credit—he seemed rather more desirable than before. At Copland's suggestion, in the spring of 1940 Carter applied for a position at Cornell University; reportedly he was on Cornell's short list, but the Cornell search committee dragged its collective feet, with the result that Carter—anxious to get on with his life—accepted a solid offer from St. John's College in Annapolis, Maryland.

Whereas Cornell at this time was a large and prestigious Ivy League university, St. John's was a small liberal-arts college famous for being one of just a handful of American institutions whose entire curriculum was—and still is—based on the Great Books program started by John Erskine at Columbia University in 1919. Considering how valuable his own humanities-oriented education had been, it is not surprising that the thirty-one-year-old Carter in 1940 fairly leaped at the chance to share comparable ideas with bright undergraduates at St. John's. And the well-versed Carter likely was flattered that the job offered to him involved the management of classes not just in music but also in mathematics, physics, philosophy, and Greek. But it did not take long for Carter to discover that committed involvement in the teaching of such classes seriously limited his time for composing.

In one of his last articles for *Modern Music*, Carter exuberantly campaigned for the inclusion of musical study—whether it be historical, theoretical, or aesthetic—in any liberal-arts curriculum.[66] At the time he wrote this article, however, Carter had already abandoned his potentially secure position at St. John's and set out on the unpredictable path of a freelance composer. After leaving St. John's in the summer of 1942 he would teach again (at the Peabody Conservatory in Baltimore from 1946 to 1948, at Columbia University in New York from 1948 to 1950), but only under prescribed conditions that allowed him to devote the bulk of his time to composing.

After his St. John's stint Carter retreated for a few months to Santa Fe, New Mexico, where against his better judgment he began to experiment with writing music "in a deliberately restricted idiom" that—unlike the *Pocahontas* score—

might somehow "be understandable to the general musical public." Among the first results of this short-lived trend was the 1942 Symphony No. 1, a three-movement work whose finale was based on a section originally penned for the *Pocahontas* sketch. The Symphony seemed well-enough received when Howard Hanson led its premiere performance in Rochester, New York, in April 1944. Still, Carter felt that despite its "directness," the Symphony No. 1—and all the other pieces that sprang from his "natural desire to write something many people could presumably grasp and enjoy easily at a time of social emergency"—was music that nevertheless "escaped the average listener."[67]

The "social emergency" to which Carter referred was, of course, the Second World War. Even though he was teaching at St. John's, Carter attempted to enlist in military service as soon as the United States entered the hostilities late in 1941, but he was rejected on grounds of health. "I had all these allergies," he recently told an interviewer, "which made me very guilty, so I tried all sorts of things to get into the war."[68] In 1943, after he and his wife resettled in New York and after their son was born, Carter very much wanted to put his knowledge of foreign languages to use in the military's intelligence units, but he failed to pass the exams that tested for aptitude in cryptography. One of the things he was asked to do but refused was spy on various German-born persons living in Manhattan; what he finally ended up doing—starting late in 1943 and continuing through the Allied forces' invasion of Normandy on 6 June 1944—was work as a musical advisor for the U.S. Office of War Information.

Along with producing documentary and instructional films, the OWI operated radio stations whose broadcasts were aimed not at fighting troops but at beleaguered civilians in Europe and North Africa. Carter worked for the overseas branch of the OWI's radio division, sometimes concocting programs built around preexisting recordings but more often supervising original recordings of "Greek, Albanian, Belgian, French, Roumanian, German, Hungarian, Norwegian, Danish, Dutch, and other musics."[69] Later in 1944, in preparation for the D-Day invasion, Carter and others on the OWI music staff prepared suitably uplifting arrangements of virtually all the European national anthems.

World War II would not end for another year, but shortly after D-Day Carter quit his OWI job and spent the rest of the summer with his wife and son in a rented house on one of the barrier islands off the south coast of Long Island. Inspired by the news of the August 1944 liberation of Paris, Carter rather quickly wrote an orchestral piece he called *Holiday Overture*. Like the 1942 Symphony No. 1 and like the handful of other works, mostly for voice, that Carter wrote after leaving his teaching position at St. John's College, the *Holiday Overture* was music that Carter sincerely hoped would be accessible to the so-called general audience. Meyer and Shreffler characterize the *Holiday Overture* as "decidedly extroverted and optimistic" yet observe, aptly, that it is "marked by a certain stylistic ambivalence."[70]

The stylistic ambivalence manifest in the *Holiday Overture* and other works from the wartime years did not escape the composer. Indeed, for Carter this ambivalence was at the very front of his attention and likely a source of constant torment. Following the lead of Copland and others who regarded World War II, as they had the Great Depression, as a mandate to write music that might somehow rally the spirits of the American citizenry, Carter tried his best between 1942 and 1945 to make his patriotic contribution. At the same time, and especially at this particular time in his life, he found it impossible to abandon the idea of producing "works that meant something to [him] as music."[71]

Carter was at first dismayed when Copland dismissed the deliberately populist and hopefully appealing *Holiday Overture* as "just another of those 'typical, complicated Carter scores.'"[72] But perhaps this brush-off confirmed a truth that Carter had been learning, albeit gradually, ever since he returned from Paris. He was beginning to realize that if he were indeed to compose music that *as music* meant something to him, that music would necessarily at least to a certain extent be "complicated."

Along with the Symphony No. 1, Carter in 1942 produced a not at all complicated song cycle for voice and piano based on three poems by Robert Frost ("Dust of Snow," "The Rose Family," "The Line Gang") and an equally simple, albeit elegant, *Elegy* for cello and piano that for years to come he would polish and rewrite for various instrumental combinations. In 1943 Carter addressed Walt Whitman's "Warble for Lilac-Time" and Hart Crane's "Voyage," the one in a setting for soprano or tenor accompanied by piano or small orchestra, the other in a setting for "medium voice" and piano, and early in 1944 he made a song of Mark Van Doren's "The Difference." Shortly after finishing the *Holiday Overture* Carter wrote two more choral pieces: late in 1944 *The Harmony of Morning*, a lyrical treatment for women's chorus and chamber orchestra of Van Doren's "Another Music," and early in 1945 a setting for a cappella mixed chorus (with optional string accompaniment) of Emily Dickinson's "Musicians Wrestle Everywhere."

Filled as it is not just with the learned devices of traditional counterpoint but also with irregular accents and conflicting meters, *Musicians Wrestle Everywhere* is easily the most complicated choral composition that Carter had written up to this time. But as Richard Franko Goldman noted more than a half century ago, compared with what was soon to come, the rhythmic problems that Carter here poses and solves—problems with which he was just starting to "wrestle"—exist only "on a small scale."[73]

Rhythmic problems on a much larger scale would be addressed in the solo instrumental work that Carter began in the summer of 1945 and finished, with the support of a grant from the Guggenheim Foundation, in January of the following year. Within a few years word of this piece had circulated through the small but influential musical community, whose collective opinion mattered a great deal, and as a result Carter's reputation rather suddenly transformed from that of just another respectable but struggling young American composer into that of a full-fledged master whose name would from then on be associated with a distinctive musical style.

As Ned Rorem would later recall, "it was [in] 1946, with his Piano Sonata, that Elliott Carter is generally agreed to have turned into Elliott Carter."[74]

2 Three Seminal Works (1945–51)

RECALLING FROM FIRSTHAND EXPERIENCE the considerable buzz that surrounded the initial performances (in 1947) and the publication (in 1948) of the Piano Sonata, Rorem was on the mark when he suggested—from the perspective of three decades later—that it had long been "generally agreed" that the Piano Sonata was the first demonstration of the uniquely "Carteresque" style. But others, writing not as actual participants in New York's fecund postwar contemporary music scene but as chronologically distanced academic observers, have contended that it was not until somewhat later that the Carteresque style first manifested itself.

In the first edition of his *Music of Elliott Carter*, which followed Rorem's statement by only five years, David Schiff identifies the landmark event as the Sonata for Cello and Piano of 1948, and he suggests that everything that came before—including the Piano Sonata—falls into the category of "creative etudes."[1] Concurring with his fellow member of an extremely small club of Carter-focused scholars, Jonathan W. Bernard observes that the Cello Sonata is indeed the first of Carter's works that "sounds distinctly different" from *all* the preceding music.[2] But Michael Cherlin, in a review of Bernard's 1997 edited collection of writings by Carter, makes the case that Carter did not express his "authentic voice" until the String Quartet No. 1 of 1951, that such earlier pieces as the 1945–46 Piano Sonata and the 1948

Cello Sonata were mere "bridge" works that allowed Carter to cross "into his first maturity."[3] And John Rockwell earlier had offered that the 1951 String Quartet represented only "the first steps" that Carter took "*toward* his mature style."[4]

Efforts to pinpoint the emergence of Carter's mature style in the long run are moot, and arguments over whether this or that piece gets the credit will inevitably devolve not so much into quibbling over technical details as into debating the relative importance of a great many details—some of them not all that technical—within special musical contexts. Still, it seems certain that it was largely because of the Piano Sonata that Carter's status changed from apprentice to journeyman composer. It seems just as certain that many on the scene, including Carter himself, indeed recognized the Piano Sonata as "a harbinger of change."[5]

When he started work on the Piano Sonata in the summer of 1945, Carter was thirty-six years old, no longer a youngster or a student, already a husband and parent, yet still somewhat dependent for financial support on an allowance from his grudging father. Surely he was aware that vis-à-vis his chosen career he was fast approaching the "now or never" point.

Considering the matter of timing from a perspective rather less crass, it should be noted that Carter's work on the Piano Sonata took place at the very moment when the United States, fresh from its explosive victory over the Japanese, was entering its psychologically troubled postwar period. As explained in the previous chapter, Carter's personal involvement in World War II was limited to a year of service as a Manhattan-based consultant to the U.S. Office of War Information. This should not suggest, however, that Carter's emotional investment in the war was ever anything less than full. Even during his years with Boulanger in the early to mid-1930s, Carter recalled, he was fairly "haunted" by "disastrous human situations" that resulted not just from the global economic depression but from the first stirrings of what eventually would be "Nazi-Fascist dictatorships."[6] And it was "the experience of living through the Second World War," Carter noted in the 1990s, "that impelled him (among others) to confront the realities of human nature and human existence once again and to take up the thread of modernism."[7]

There is no reason to doubt that Carter's emotions, although experienced from positions of relative safety, were wholly genuine. But even if Carter had somehow managed to immunize himself against the horrors transpiring in the European and Pacific theaters, it would have been virtually impossible for him to remain aloof from America's immediate postwar anxieties. As early as December 1945, a mere four months after the war's end, the Nobel Prize–winning Finnish agriculturalist A. I. Virtanen caused "scandal and great uproar" and prompted denunciations by the international press by casually remarking to a journalist that he simply did not trust the Soviet Union.[8] The so-called cold war did not "officially" begin until 1 April 1948, when Soviet ground troops began their blockade of the sectors of Berlin that since the end of the war had been under the control of France, Great Britain, and the United States, and it did not reach its first peak until the mid-1950s, when virtually the entire U.S. citizenship was racked by fears of Communist infiltration and all-out thermonuclear war. Among internationally minded Americans who paid close attention to the news, however, fear was in the air even as Carter toiled over his Piano Sonata.

In a reflection on the situation of American composers in the aftermath of World War II, Martin Boykan observed that Carter's post-1945 music was "electrifying to the postwar generation" not just because of its high quality but also because it was simply "the kind of work that was very much needed and desired." It spoke for the serious-minded America of the 1950s in much the same way that Stravinsky's *Rite of Spring* had spoken for the Europe of a half century ago; it was "of importance to the postwar generation not only because of its artistic power, but also because it provide[d] a moral lesson."[9] Although Boykan here was writing specifically about Carter's 1951 String Quartet No. 1, the assessment applies as well—at least to an extent—to the Cello Sonata and the Piano Sonata.

Just as the timing circa 1945 was right, in the limited context of his personal career, for Carter to produce music that might identify him once and for all not as a neophyte but as a mature composer, so the timing was right, in the broad context of midcentury cultural-political developments, for American composers in general to again "take up the thread of modernism" and produce music much more forceful than what for the previous decade had been the norm. Thoughts of this sort of timing—apropos of both the private course of his career and the grandly public march of history—doubtless crossed Carter's mind when he embarked upon the Piano Sonata. But also on his mind circa 1945 was another sort of timing, one relative only to the inner workings of a musical composition.

Deep into the book-length interview with Edwards, after discussion of various of his works to date, Carter—in response to a question about the degree to which "the sense of musical motion" contributed to coherence in a composition—tellingly stated that "any technical or esthetic consideration of music really must *start* with the matter of time." In Carter's view, most analysts did not approach music this way; instead of regarding the various sections of music as "*transitive* steps" that lead from one moment to another, he said, they regard them as static elements. And Carter emphasized that, in order to fully comprehend not just his music but virtually any music, "all the materials of music have to be considered in relation to their projection in time, and by time, of course, I mean not visually measured 'clock-time,' but the medium through which (or way in which) we perceive, understand, and experience events. Music deals with this experiential kind of time, and its vocabulary must be organized by a musical syntax that takes direct account of, and thus can play on, the listener's 'time-sense.'"[10]

In a 1995 essay titled "Elliott Carter and the Modern Meaning of Time," Bernard mentions Carter's "great epiphany about time," after which Carter "began to work, somewhat tentatively at first and then with increasing confidence, with various 'simultaneous streams of different things going on together' as well as [with] closely interleaved, mutually interruptive continuities."[11] Bernard's essay is a lucid account not just of the various ways with which Carter has dealt with time in all his mature music but also of how Carter's ideas evolved and, especially, how they relate to early influences from the fields of film, dance, and literature. But the reference is cryptic, for Bernard never explains when or where—or under what circumstances—this "great epiphany" took place.

As can be gleaned from the interview with Edwards and from Carter's various writings that have specifically to do with time, the epiphany was hardly so dramatic as what Saul experienced on the road to Damascus. Nevertheless, as Carter told Edwards, the reassessment of time vis-à-vis music seems to have happened rather quickly. Presumably referring to the period during which he halfheartedly worked on the *Holiday Overture*, Carter said that the role of time in music "began to seem important to me around 1944, when I suddenly realized that, at least in my own education, people had always been consciously concerned only with this or that peculiar local rhythmic combination or sound-texture or novel harmony and had forgotten that the really interesting thing about music is the time of it—the way it goes along."[12]

Using a phrase that indeed suggests a bolt-from-the-blue enlightenment, Carter told Edwards that it "struck him" that

> despite the newness and variety of the post-tonal musical vocabulary, most modern pieces generally "went along" in an all-too-uniform way on their higher architectonic levels. That is, it seemed to me that, while we had heard every imaginable kind of harmonic and timbral combination, and while there had been a degree of rhythmic innovation on the *local* level in the music of Stravinsky, Bartók, Varèse, and Ives particularly, nonetheless the way

all this went together at the next higher and succeeding higher rhythmic levels remained in the orbit of what had begun to seem to me the rather limited rhythmic routine of previous Western music.[13]

As noted in the previous chapter, Carter as a high-school student had been interested in the music of Indonesia and India, and after his first year in college he spent a summer in Tunisia making transcriptions of Arabic music. In 1944, he told Edwards, he "once again—after many years' hiatus—took up interest" in the rhythmic elements of these and other non-Western musics.[14] He studied anew how matters of time had been dealt with not just in the music of Scriabin and Ives but also in the music of the early Quattrocento, and he drew useful ideas from Henry Cowell's 1930 *New Musical Resources.*[15] One of the first results in his own music, Carter said, was "the way of evolving rhythms and continuities now called 'metric modulation.'"[16]

For decades a cliché in discussions of Carter's mature music, the term *metric modulation* seems to have been coined not by Carter but by Richard Franko Goldman in a 1951 assessment of several of Carter's most recent compositions.[17] For that matter, metric modulation's underlying concept was hardly an invention of Carter. As Edwards points out in an illuminating footnote that surely met with Carter's approval, "there is nothing new about metric modulation but the name." He explains:

> To limit brief mention of [metric modulation's] derivations in notated Western music: it is implicit in the rhythmic procedures of late fourteenth-century French music, as it is in music of the fifteenth and sixteenth centuries that uses hemiola and other ways of alternating meters, especially duple and triple. From then on, since early sets of variations like those of Byrd and Bull started a tradition of tempo relationships between movements, metric modulation began to relate movements of one piece together, as can be seen in many works of Beethoven, not only in the variations of Op. 111, but in many places where *doppio movimento* and other terms are used to indicate tempo relationships. In fact, at that very time, the metronome was invented, which establishes relationships between all tempi.[18]

The hemiola mentioned by Edwards derives from the Greek word *hēmiolos*, which means "the whole and its half." Music theorists in ancient Greece used the term primarily to describe the 3:2 ratio that results in the harmonic or melodic interval known as the perfect fifth; European theorists in the fifteenth and sixteenth centuries used the same term—and its Latin equivalent, *sesquialtera*—to describe the 3:2 ratio between "perfect" and "imperfect" meters, that is, meters that featured strong pulses divided into three smaller pulses and meters that featured equally strong pulses divided into only two smaller pulses. A modern form of hemiola could be notated as a change from $\frac{6}{8}$ meter to $\frac{3}{4}$, or vice versa. In either case, the smaller pulses (eighth notes) retain a constant value while the strong pulses change, in the first instance, from groupings of three small pulses (i.e., dotted quarter notes) to groupings of two (i.e., quarter notes). If the eighth note had a constant value of, say, 240 per minute, the hemiola would involve a sudden quickening from a pace of 80 dotted quarter notes per minute to a rate of 120 quarter notes per minute.

In essence, Carter's metric modulations are extensions of the same basic principle, one that had been theorized aplenty during the Renaissance and that manifested itself often in the work of nineteenth-century European composers who sought to infuse their concert works with the "raw spirit" of folk music. But whereas metric modulations in the music of, for example, Brahms and Dvořák were for the most part limited to the simple 3:2 ratio, Carter took the idea many steps further, eventually working with such complex ratios as 7:3, 8:3, 15:8, and 21:20. Carter's metric modulations, which, in fact, he prefers to call "temporal modulations," are sometimes obvious, sometimes extremely subtle. Always, though, they are different in both concept and effect from mere accelerations or decelerations; they are indeed changes of rates of musical flow, but invariably they are both instantaneous and systematic.

Carter said that his personal method of metric modulation was first "worked out" in the 1948 Cello Sonata.[19] But the trail toward this "working out" was already being blazed in the 1945–46 Piano Sonata, and the thought of setting forth on such an adventurous trail was surely in Carter's mind even as he composed his harmonically bold yet rhythmically quite traditional *Holiday Overture.*

Speaking from the perspective of 1971, Carter told Edwards that what contemporary music in general needs is not just inventive "raw materials" but a context in which such materials might "evolve during the course of a work in a sharply meaningful way," a context in which it would be clear enough that "everything that happens" to the materials "happens *as* and *when* it does in relation to everything else."[20] Carter said that he felt very strongly about this, because "ever since 1944" he realized that

> ultimately the matter of musical time is vastly more important than the particulars or the novelty of the musical vocabulary, and that the morphological elements of any music owe their musical effect almost entirely to their specific "placing" in the musical time-continuity, just as perfectly ordinary and familiar details in a work of literature, like, say, the Library in Borges's *Library of Babel,* or the cockroach in Kafka's *Metamorphosis,* or the events (each commonplace enough) in K's life in [Kafka's] *The Castle,* only take on the peculiar

and gripping significance they have as a result of the manner and order in which they are juxtaposed and combined in the literary time-continuity.[21]

After the *Holiday Overture* and the two choral pieces from 1944 and 1945 (*The Harmony of Morning* and *Musicians Wrestle Everywhere*), Carter embarked wholeheartedly on his still ongoing exploration of the effects of placement of small-scale gestures within large-scale schemes of "musical time-continuity." His only relapses into traditional modes of rhythmic organization came in 1947 in the form of a one-act ballet titled *The Minotaur* (commissioned by Lincoln Kirstein for the Ballet Society company that he had founded the year before) and *Emblems*, a setting of a text by Allen Tate for piano-accompanied men's chorus (commissioned by G. Wallace Woodworth for the Harvard Glee Club).[22] But these two examples of conservative backpeddling, it is important to note, were composed *before* Carter's 1945–46 Piano Sonata attracted public acclaim.

Piano Sonata (1945–46)

Completed in January 1946, the sonata was written for Carter's Harvard classmate Ralph Kirkpatrick. Doubtless to Carter's chagrin, Kirkpatrick rejected it at least in part on the grounds that the music seemed too "awfully intellectualized," but other pianists soon enough rose to the challenge.[23] The piece received its premiere at the hands of Webster Aitken on 16 February 1947 in a concert that took place at New York's Frick Museum and was aired "live" by the Municipal Broadcasting System; subsequent readings were given by James Sykes in Times Hall on 5 March 1947, by Aitken again in Town Hall on 12 March 1948, and by Beveridge Webster at the Hunter College Playhouse on 2 May 1948. It was Aitken's 1948 reprise performance—several months before the sonata's publication by both Music Press, Inc., and Mercury Music—that generated the first reviews.

The sonata "might just possibly be a work for the repertory," wrote Virgil Thomson, the composer who, like Carter, had studied with Boulanger and who since 1940 had held the influential position of chief music critic for the *New York Herald Tribune*. "This is a sustained piece full of power and brilliance. Its relatively quiet moments, though a shade reminiscent of Copland and Stravinsky, are not entirely, in feeling, derivative; and as figuration they are quite personal. The brilliant toccatalike passages, of which there are many, are to my ear completely original. I have never heard the sound of them or felt the feeling of them before. They are most impressive indeed."[24]

Likewise positive was the reviewer for the *New York Times*, who noted that "contemporary contrapuntal style was exhibited in full flower in Mr. Carter's opus":

"Uncompromising in their exhaustive development of material, the two movements never relaxed their grip on the audience. One never fails to be impressed with this composer's variety of textures. With his sounds of ripplings, bells, echoes and harp-like arpeggios, he controls intensity as if it were light through a fabric. There is always a sense of energetic movement and direction."[25]

It is hardly surprising that both reviewers remarked on the "sound[s]" of the piece. Surely one of the most immediate impressions any listener gets from the Piano Sonata, especially when it is experienced in a live performance, is of its panoply of sonorities. As Carter explained in a 1948 account written for Edgard Varèse, the sonata was "conceived in a style that is purely idiomatic for the modern concert grand piano and employs a large range of techniques that are peculiar to that instrument."[26] The range of pianistic techniques—which includes not just numerous modes of attack and a wide variety of chordal spacings but also, and perhaps most aurally intriguing, pedal operations that exploit the grand piano's capacity for resonance and sustained harmonics—is large, indeed.

It is likewise not surprising that the reviewers commented on the propulsive "feeling" of the sonata's many toccata-like passages and its overall "energetic movement and direction." These, too, are qualities of the Piano Sonata that are likely to be observed by an attentive first-time listener. But what the sonata's early reviewers overlooked, and what still eludes the attention of many listeners of Carter's mature music, is the composition's temporal elements.

Continuing the introduction of the account he provided Varèse, Carter noted that the sonata is a clear manifestation of his new interest in "the plastic flow of music and in contrasting rates of change . . . in the time plan of music, and in the modeling of phrases and sections and their interconnections, rather than in the discovery of novel momentary effects."[27] At the end of the document, in an addendum labeled "Artistic Credo," Carter declared: "As a composer I am primarily concerned with the contrasts and changes of character in music, in plastic flow, in motion from one point to another, and with the expression of feelings as they change smoothly or abruptly, one commenting [on], amplifying, or denying the other. The interesting operation of cause and effect, of transformation in time, of the whole sense of flow reveals itself in changes of harmony, of rhythm and texture rather than in static repetitions. My music is essentially a kinetic projection of ideas, using perspectives of time."[28]

Certain key phrases in these statements—"contrasting rates of change," "motion from one point to another," the expression of feelings that change "smoothly or abruptly"—immediately conjure up concrete sonic images. Others of them—the "plastic flow" and the "time plan" of music, a "kinetic projection of ideas" that uses "perspectives of time"—at first seem merely poetic. Taken together, however, these resonant phrases go a long way toward articulating the very essence not just of the Piano Sonata but of almost everything that came later. The general effect of Carter's "Carteresque" music perhaps defies explanation and is perhaps at best describable only by means of metaphors. Nevertheless, the methods by which Carter for more than sixty years has achieved his characteristic Carteresque effect are always attributable, in one creative way or another, to temporal procedures comparable to those that Carter so eagerly shared with Varèse.

In a radio commentary delivered circa 1960 Carter said that the opening of the Piano Sonata "is the first passage in my works that is not primarily thematic. Its central idea comes from the total sound of the piano writing."[29] But thematic writing certainly makes up the bulk of the sonata, and Carter, in the analysis he gave to Varèse, did not hesitate to point out the various themes and theme groups. Carter's statements, developments, and recapitulations of clearly identifiable themes, and his deliberate fugal treatment of one of those themes in the second of the two movements, has led some critics to argue that in terms of its large-scale structure the Piano Sonata was not really all that new. Be that as it may, in terms of its small-scale gestures the sonata was definitely a bold move forward.

Sonata for Cello and Piano (1948)

In the fall of 1946, after the Piano Sonata had been completed but well in advance of its first public performance, Carter accepted a teaching position at the Peabody Conservatory in Baltimore, Maryland. At around the same time, he took on the herculean—and emotionally difficult—task of sorting through the manuscripts of Charles Ives as an initial step toward what would eventually be performing editions of Ives's orchestral music. Based in New York through all this, Carter in 1947 composed the ballet *The Minotaur* and the choral piece *Emblems* described above, and early in 1948 he completed a woodwind quintet that represents the last of his efforts in the neoclassical style.

In the fall of 1948 Carter began teaching, closer to home, in the humanities department at Columbia University. But before Carter accepted the post at Columbia he had already embarked upon the work for piano and cello that apparently he had been contemplating in the abstract for several years. With the virtuosic abilities of cellist Bernard Greenhouse specifically in mind, Carter began writing his Sonata for Cello and Piano in the late summer of 1948 and completed it in December of that year; the first public performance, by Greenhouse and pianist Anthony Makas, took place in New York's Town Hall on 27 February 1950.

As noted early in this chapter, some commentators locate Carter's stylistic breakthrough as early as the 1945–46 Piano Sonata, while others find the real emergence of the Carteresque style only in the 1951 String Quartet No. 1. But it seems that the majority of serious writers on Carter, in their efforts to identify the singularly momentous turning point, have focused neither on the Piano Sonata nor on the String Quartet but, rather, on the Cello Sonata. What is it, one might wonder, that makes the 1948 Cello Sonata seem so special?

A search for the answer to that question might begin with the obvious fact that the Cello Sonata is scored not for one instrument but two. In the "Artistic Credo" that he appended to his analysis of the Piano Sonata, Carter clearly articulated his interest in "character in music" and the idea of playing one "expression" of character against another, not just for the sake of achieving moment-to-moment contrast but for rhetorical purposes.[30] Notwithstanding the wide range of sonority-related techniques that Carter employed in the Piano Sonata, in any work for a single instrument the dialectic almost by definition must result primarily from different character-rich statements coming one after the other. In a work for more than one instrument, on the other hand, statements of markedly differing character—statements that, for example, might somehow comment on, amplify, or deny one another—can easily be presented at the same time.

Carter has often addressed this fundamentally simple concept that has manifested itself in countless complex ways in virtually all his mature music. But one of his most cogent comments on the matter—especially interesting because it illuminates a change of thinking that took place *between* his work on the Piano Sonata and the Cello Sonata—is to be found in a fairly obscure publication issued in 1984 by the U.S. Library of Congress. Belatedly celebrating Carter's seventieth birthday, the eighty-seven-page brochure—titled *The Musical Languages of Elliott Carter*—featured in its second half a detailed catalog of the library's Carter-related holdings and an equally detailed bibliography of Carter-related writings to date. The brochure's first half was given over to pianist Charles Rosen, who offered a pair of brief lecture-based essays and an interview with the composer.

In the interview, Rosen, who by this time had positioned himself as a champion performer of Carter's keyboard music, inquired as to how the "actual [musical] language" of the Piano Sonata related to the instrument for which the piece had been written. Tellingly, Carter replied that before the Piano Sonata he had thought of instrumental music largely in the abstract, as an array of pitched sounds whose rhythmic relationships and internal voice leadings needed to be carefully worked out well before the sounds were assigned to specific members of an ensemble. Before the Piano Sonata, Carter told Rosen, he had only composed, aside from his choral essays, "what you might call works conceived as music that had to be instrumented. There was a prior thought about the music but not about the instrument[s] . . . that [were] going to play it." It was not until the Piano Sonata, Carter said, that he tried to "achieve individualization" of a particular instrument, and then "it was not long before I began to feel that this was such an interesting idea—that I could create conflicts between two kinds of instruments with different kinds of expression and ways of being played. From that time on my works played various characters off against each other, and the form of the works derived from this interplay between different instruments."[31]

Interplay between different instruments surely lies at the heart of the 1948 Cello Sonata, but in its most striking moments it is hardly interplay of the sort one encounters in the cello sonatas of, say, Beethoven or Brahms. In those earlier works, interplay occurs most often in developmental sections, and usually it involves the two instruments rapidly taking turns at presenting fragments of a single musical idea. Carter's sonata likewise features episodes during which the two instruments focus in one way or another on a single idea, but it also features interplay in which *multiple* ideas, differentiated at the very least by gestural affect, are offered simultaneously.

Cautioning readers not to jump too quickly to conclusions, Jonathan Bernard is careful to point out that "the feature of simultaneous contrast is not exactly pervasive" in the Cello Sonata, that "it is evident really only at the beginning and the end of the work."[32] Indeed, this feature is most obviously evident in the first movement's fifty or so opening measures, a passage written *after* the rest of the sonata had been more or less finished. While David Schiff excitedly writes that this opening passage represents Carter's effort "to tie the sonata together and state its novel rhythmic, harmonic and formal ideas [all] at once" in a way that "dramatically announces a new-found musical world," Bernard plays it safe by stating only that the Cello Sonata is the first of Carter's works "in which the idea of 'simultaneous streams' is realized to any appreciable extent."[33]

Carter confirmed as much in a 1968 interview with Benjamin Boretz, but he also suggested—contrary to Bernard's observation—that "overlapping speeds" provided him with an "underlying pattern for the *entire* work."[34] And he offered a synopsis that describes not only the Cello Sonata's technical means but also its expressive ends:

> After the first measure, the piano starts a regular beat, like a clock ticking, against which the cello plays an expressive melodic line in an apparently free manner without any clear coordination with the piano beat. This establishes the two completely different planes of musical character. The entire form of this piece then consists of bringing these two instru-

ments into various relationships with one another. There are developments, continuations, of this contrast between the two instruments, not, in this particular case, so much in terms of intervallic structure, but more in oppositions of character. So the piano and the cello are kept distinct throughout most of this work. I don't know how the conception ever originated; it was actually the first time I had ever had the idea. I carried it out much further in 1951 in my First String Quartet and then in subsequent works, but the Cello Sonata was the first time I tried to make a piece that had two contrasting aspects that could be heard as one totality.[35]

Like the account of the Piano Sonata that Carter had given to Varèse, this succinct description of the Cello Sonata contains key phrases (e.g., "different planes of musical character" and "oppositions of character," "contrasting aspects that could be heard as one totality") that before long applied to almost everything that Carter would produce.

String Quartet No. 1 (1951)

From a distance of more than six decades, and benefiting from hindsight that takes in all the music that Carter has produced since the early 1950s, perhaps it makes the most sense to regard the opening of the Cello Sonata not so much as a passage that "dramatically announces a new-found musical world" but simply as yet another step along Carter's evolutionary path. In marked contrast, the String Quartet No. 1 seems truly a declaration of independence.

The 1945–46 Piano Sonata was written specifically for Ralph Kirkpatrick, and the 1948 Cello Sonata was written specifically for cellist Bernard Greenhouse. Significantly, the 1951 String Quartet was written for no one in particular, after Carter had "decided for once to write a work very interesting to myself, and to say to hell with the public and the performers, too."[36] Moreover, the quartet was written for the most part during a year of retreat from the busyness of New York that Carter spent—supported by a grant from the Guggenheim Foundation—in the relative isolation and "undisturbed quiet" of Tucson, Arizona.[37]

Carter's statement about saying "to hell" with both the public and the performers should not be taken as an expression of bitterness. It is true that Kirkpatrick, for whom the Piano Sonata had been written, begged off after confronting the music's "awfully intellectualized" content, but other pianists readily accepted the sonata's challenges, and Greenhouse had no problems with the cello piece. Both works generated favorable reviews in the New York press, and even as Carter labored over his string quartet, both of them were being committed to vinyl.[38] Carter in the early postwar period was indeed writing music that many listeners likely would have construed as "difficult," but this was nevertheless music that the market seemed to bear, and he had little reason to complain about the reception it received from the sophisticated audience at which it was aimed.

Still, Carter in 1950 felt the need to escape the expectations of audiences and critics and to compose a piece that, for no other reason than to please himself, "carried out completely the various ideas [he] had at that time about the form of music, about texture and harmony—about everything."[39] The quartet was "written largely for my own satisfaction and grew out of an effort to understand myself," Carter recalled.[40] He did not deliberately write it "so that it would be unplayable," he said, but as he worked on it he doubted that it would ever be performed.[41]

Whereas the Cello Sonata is remarkable for being the first of Carter's works to explore the simultaneous presentation of contrasting musical ideas differentiated largely by gesture, the String Quartet No. 1, which was performed by the Walden Quartet in New York in 1953 and by the Parrenin Quartet in Rome in 1954, is remarkable for being the first of Carter's works to involve simultaneous ideas differentiated not just by gesture but also by speed. As had been the case with the Cello Sonata, the quartet's strikingly new feature is most evident in the opening and closing sections. As Carter explained in a 1960 article titled "Shop Talk by an American Composer," "If you listen to or look at any part of the first or last movement of my First String Quartet, you will find that there is a constant change of pulse. This is caused by an overlapping of speeds. Say, one part in triplets will enter against another part in quintuplets and the quintuplets will fade into the background and the triplets will establish a new speed that will become the springboard for another such operation."[42]

Carter attested that "the structure of such speeds is correlated *throughout* the work," but Bernard has argued that the "application [of this procedure] is still fairly limited at this point of [Carter's] development," that the establishment of simultaneous speeds "is usually a matter of only a few measures, and quite often not all parts are included."[43] Nevertheless, the several occasions that indeed feature a full array of different speeds are most impressive. The first of these is heard at measure 22 of the quartet's opening Fantasia movement. All four parts are notated in $\frac{4}{4}$ meter and assigned a metronome marking of 120 quarter notes per minute, but only the relatively simple cello part, for a while, actually *moves* at this rate; playing tied notes, each of which encompasses a time span of five sixteenth notes, the second violin moves at the slower rate of 96 pulses per minute, and the high-pitched first violin, assigned long tied notes comprising two quarter notes and one third of a triplet, moves at the very slow rate of 36 pulses per minute; the viola, when it enters after a three-measure rest, plays quarter-note triplets whose articulations—relating to the cello line in the manner of the hemiola discussed early in this chapter—occur at the rate of 180 per minute.[44]

Temporal machinations of this sort grew more and more complex as the decades rolled along, and as a result some critics and performers—apparently able to do the math but otherwise immune to the real gist of Carter's music—have come to believe that the Carter aesthetic has to do primarily with so-called metric modulation. But commentators who focus exclusively on the rhythmic aspects of Carter's music tend to miss the point of the overtly dramatic "changes of character in music" that Carter had been trying to realize ever since his 1945–46 Piano Sonata. They miss the point, too, of the harmonic means by which Carter lent integrity to his breakthrough pieces even as he sought, with contrasting gestures and rates of musical flow, to differentiate one instrumental voice from another.

In both the Cello Sonata and the Quartet No. 1, the diverse parts are "heard as one totality" chiefly because their obvious differences in character are balanced by a subtle consistency in their pitch content. This concept—one that has rhythmically dissimilar components infused with an underlying harmonic unity—would play an important role in all the music that Carter wrote from this point up until 1959. The 1959 String Quartet No. 2 would feature different pitch sets for each of its four component parts. But the works that came before this—along with the String Quartet No. 1, most notably, the 1952 Sonata for Flute, Oboe, Cello, and Harpsichord, and the 1953–55 Variations for Orchestra, but also the 1949 Eight Etudes and a Fantasy for Woodwind Quartet and even the 1950 Six Pieces for Kettledrums—all followed the model of the Cello Sonata and used a pervasive construction of pitches as a method of bringing together materials that, on first listen, seem in many ways very different.

For example, the Cello Sonata opens with the piano sounding four simultaneous pitches (in the left hand F-sharp and A, in the right hand A-sharp and E-sharp) and then thickening the mix with two more pitches (D-sharp followed by B, each played by both hands in octaves).[45] The result is a collection of tones that, whether arrayed simultaneously or successively, Carter has long been comfortable in identifying simply as a "chord" but that most music theorists today, in discussing nontonal music, would likely call a "pitch-class set." This specific set of six pitch classes serves as what Schiff colorfully describes as a "primal sonority" whose intervallic ingredients "define the nature of the musical exploration that follows." It in effect presents all of the work's "genetic matter," but it is no more the composition's "theme" than "a man's chromosomes would be his vocation." Indeed, Schiff continues, "in the Cello Sonata, for the first time in Carter's music, such genetic structure decisively replaces thematic exposition, and transformation now takes the place of development and recapitulation."[46]

Although its exploration was decidedly more complex, the basic "genetic matter" of the String Quartet No. 1 was in fact simpler than that of the Cello Sonata. It was just a four-note chord, or pitch-class set, whose component pitches when linked in pairs yielded one—but *only* one—of each of the six possible musical intervals. As Carter explained in his "Shop Talk" article, the "all-interval" tetrachord used throughout the String Quartet No. 1 comprises the pitches E, F, A-flat, and B-flat (i.e., the pitch-class set nowadays identified as [0,1,4,6]).[47] There is only one other four-note chord whose two-by-two combinations result in all six intervals (starting on the same pitch as the aforementioned array, this could be spelled E–F–G–B and identified as the pitch-class set [0,1,3,7]). But this other all-interval tetrachord minus just one of its component pitches would be equivalent to a minor or (in inversion) major triad. In later works, starting with the 1959 String Quartet No. 2, Carter would indeed accept and creatively work with the traditional tonal implications of the [0,1,3,7] tetrachord. But throughout the 1951 String Quartet No. 1 he opted only for the more ambiguous [0,1,4,6] configuration. This "key" four-note chord, Carter explained, "is not used at *every* moment in the work," but it nevertheless "occurs frequently enough, especially in important places, to function, I hope, as a formative factor."[48]

The all-interval tetrachord, to be sure, is not the only "formative factor" in the String Quartet No. 1. The work's overall plan, Carter wrote, was inspired by Jean Cocteau's 1930 film *Le sang d'une poète*, in which

> the entire dreamlike action is framed by an interrupted slow-motion shot of a tall brick chimney in an empty lot being dynamited. Just as the chimney begins to fall apart, the shot is broken off and the entire movie follows, after which the shot of the chimney is resumed at the point it left off. . . . A similar interrupted continuity is employed in this quartet's starting with a cadenza for cello alone that is continued by the first violin alone at the very end. On one level, I interpret Cocteau's idea (and my own) as establishing the difference between external time (measured by the falling chimney, or the cadenza) and internal dream time (the main body of the work)—the dream time lasting but a moment of external time but from the dreamer's point of view a long stretch.[49]

Whether perceived by a listener as representing "dream time" or "external time," the String Quartet No. 1 in performance lasts between forty-five and fifty minutes, a duration that prompted an early Carter champion to describe it as being, on the clock, "very long." But the same critic also described the quartet as possessing "a dark intensity and power" and of being, organically, both "dense and unified."[50]

The work's pervasive unity—likely to be not so much noticed as inwardly *felt* by any listener—derives in large part from the deliberately limited harmonic language and the intricate metric linkages described above. The work's formidable density—doubtless in the foreground of attention even of listeners who have experienced the quartet on numerous occasions—derives not just from the four instruments' almost constant disparity in "character" but also from propulsive rhythms that can be perceived only when the markedly different pulses of the four instruments are grasped in toto and from a rich set of references (mere allusions to Ruth Crawford's 1931 String Quartet and the 1928 String Quartet No. 4 of Béla Bartók, actual quotations from Charles Ives's 1902–8 Violin Sonata No. 1 and Conlon Nancarrow's *Rhythm Study No. 1* for player piano). The listener's perception of density results as well from the fact that in the String Quartet No. 1, as in many of his later works, Carter deliberately blurs the music's internal boundaries: there are discernible pauses, yet they occur not between movements but only within movements.

Instead of the "go-and-stop" format of traditional works for the concert hall, William Brandt observes, the quartet gives the impression of a "continuous music narrative."[51] But it is a narrative modeled not on mainstream novels, in which storytelling is for the most part straightforwardly linear, but on the decidedly avant-garde novels that Carter came to know during his youth and early adulthood. Not only does the overall plan of the quartet resemble "that of many 'circular' works of modern literature," Carter recalled, "but the interlocked presentation of ideas parallels many characteristic devices found in Joyce and others—the controlled 'stream of consciousness,' the 'epiphany,' the many uses of punctuation, of grammatical ambiguities, including the use of quotation."[52] Indeed, as Schiff writes in the first edition of his book on Carter, the String Quartet No. 1 was "probably the first musical composition of [the twentieth] century to rival the formal daring of Eliot, Joyce, Proust or Eisenstein."[53]

Notwithstanding this bold nonlinear structure, and notwithstanding the intricate pitch and rhythmic organization that governs not just the 1951 String Quartet No. 1 but also the 1948 Cello Sonata and the 1945–46 Piano Sonata, what the listener likely draws from these seminal works is an experience less intellectual than visceral.

In his 1960 "Shop Talk" article Carter dutifully explained his rhythmic procedures to date but urged readers not to think of them as "a trick or a formula," and he stated clearly that he never considered rhythmic devices of any sort to be "an integral part of [his] musical personality."[54] Sixteen years later, in an essay titled "Music and the Time Screen," he as much as apologized for having offered technical details pertaining to the pitch and rhythmic content of various of his works. With apparent resignation, Carter wrote: "To have indulged in the foregoing explanations and to be faced with the prospect of their being used as a substitute for listening to the music itself and fed into the general hopper of American education, artistic statements—later to be ground up and to come out as undifferentiated fodder to be forcibly fed to the young and permanently regurgitated at exams—is apparently the terrible fate of such efforts as these and the disheartening result of America's ambivalence toward the arts."[55]

The British musicologist Wilfrid Mellers in 1964 compared Carter to Beethoven, observing that both composers are "intensely dramatic artist[s] . . . concerned with the drama of the inner life." Although his comments apply to Carteresque music in general, Mellers here was writing specifically of the Cello Sonata, the work that he—like Schiff and Bernard—singles out as the first of Carter's mature compositions. In the Cello Sonata, Mellers writes, "the drama is inherent in the nature of the instruments themselves." The instruments at first are presented in opposition, but eventually their "incompatibility" of timbre, attack, and sustaining power "becomes a virtue, for they are 'personified' as independent identities which have to seek a relationship."[56]

Paul Griffiths, a British writer who eventually penned the libretto for Carter's only opera, in 1995 similarly labeled Carter as first and foremost a musical dramatist. For Griffiths, as for Cherlin, Carter's "signal of arrival in new terrain" was not the Cello Sonata but the String Quartet No. 1, a work in which musical change—"deliberately engineered and motivated"—is not just "a symptom" of innovative techniques but "the prime subject" of the discourse. Perhaps in an effort to forestall "programmatic" interpretations of this and other of Carter's compositions, Griffiths emphasizes that the protagonists whose relationships evolve over the course of the quartet are invariably "abstract" characters, defined not by mood or psychological state but only by such purely musical materials as pitch content and rate of pulse. Writing of the String Quartet No. 1 in particular but following Mellers's lead and in effect commenting on Carteresque music in general, Griffiths concludes that Carter is "a dramatist . . . not of human figures" but, rather, "of energies."[57]

This is an apt summary, yet it prompts one to wonder about the nature of the conflicting "energies" that first manifest themselves in the Piano Sonata and that ever since have been the dramatis personae of Carter's music. These various energies are of course describable in technical terms and capable of being represented—with far more accuracy than language can hope to offer—in charts and annotated musical examples. To focus only on their musical content, however, would be to deny these energies their effect as well as their affect. Even the most clinical analysts, one suspects, would grant that each of Carter's musical energies has a certain *feel*, evident enough when its constituent materials are heard in isolation and all the more palpable when presented in combination or juxtaposition with energies that are in some way different.

Griffiths rightly argues that the sharply differentiated "characters" in Carter's musical dramas are not analogous to specific "human figures," but Mellers just as rightly argues that Carter, like Beethoven, has long focused on the drama of the "inner life." The content of this inner life—the wellspring of the music's energies—is perhaps something that, as Carter has said of his motivations for composing, "cannot be put into words."[58] But to be ineffable does not mean to be insubstantial. The potent energies that swirl through Carter's music are very real, and they have to do with matters fundamentally, and absolutely, human.

3 Maturity (1950–80)

CARTER'S STRING QUARTET NO. 1 was written over a ten-month period in 1950–51 during which the composer was supported by a fellowship from the Guggenheim Foundation. Work on his 1945–46 Piano Sonata had been funded by the same philanthropic organization, and in 1950 Carter benefited not just from the second Guggenheim Fellowship but also from a small grant from the National Institute of Arts and Letters. Along with these awards, Carter at midcentury had several composition prizes to his credit: his 1937 choral piece *To Music* earned top honors in a competition sponsored by the WPA Federal Music Project in cooperation with the Columbia Broadcasting Corporation, the Columbia Phonograph Company, and the publisher Carl Fischer, Inc.; the suite from his 1939 *Pocahontas* ballet received the Juilliard School of Music's publication prize; and his 1944 *Holiday Overture* won first prize in an Independent Music Publishers' Association contest.

By September 1951, when he completed the landmark string quartet that he said was conceived and executed to satisfy no one but himself, Carter already owned a résumé that included not just prizes and awards but also favorably reviewed performances, commissions, publications, and even recordings. Because of these various successes, combined with the regular appearance over a ten-year period of his byline in the journal *Modern Music*, Carter in the early 1950s hardly lacked for recognition. Yet as impressive as all this might have seemed to a middle-aged composer who felt that he had only recently discovered his "true voice," the sum total of accolades that Carter had acquired up to this point counts almost as nothing compared to the recognition that would come his way shortly after the quartet's European premiere.

As noted in the previous chapter, Carter doubted that his String Quartet No. 1 would ever be performed. It was to his surprise, then, that the piece was taken up by the Walden Quartet and given a first performance at Columbia University's McMillin Theatre on 26 February 1953. Doubtless it was even more to his surprise when a few months later the piece was awarded first prize in the Liège Concours international de composition pour quatour à cordes. Since the Liège competition was limited to works that had yet to be performed, Carter had to turn down both the honor and the cash prize. This peculiar circumstance was newsworthy, and so were the facts that Carter's piece was apparently so difficult that its private reading in Liège necessitated the use of a conductor and that the Boston-based Koussevitzky Foundation, which sponsored the Liège competition, made up for Carter's loss of the prize money (40,000 Belgian francs) not just by writing him a check for $800 but also by granting him a commission.[1]

As a result of widespread press reports, European aficionados of contemporary music had heard quite a bit about Carter's piece before any of them actually heard it—in the expert hands of the Paris-based Parrenin Quartet—in Rome on 11 April 1954 during a concert that was part of the "Music in the Twentieth Century" festival sponsored by the Congress for Cultural Freedom in cooperation with the Italian national radio system and the Geneva-based European Center of Culture.[2]

The 1954 Rome festival was instigated and managed by Carter's old friend Nicolas Nabokov. By the time of the festival Carter had been living and working in Rome for more than a half year as a result of his being awarded the American Academy's prestigious Prix de Rome by a jury that included not just Nabokov but also Carter's longtime supporter Aaron Copland and his former teacher Walter Piston, and for months in advance of the festival Carter had taken full advantage of the opportunity to forge personal relationships with many of Europe's most prominent composers and critics.

This is not to suggest that Carter's success in Europe had anything to do with pulling strings by him or anyone else. It is simply to say that Carter, ever since his return to the United States after his studies with Boulanger, had the good sense to play his cards smartly and that in the spring of 1954 he had the good fortune to be in the right place at the right time with what seemed to be exactly the right kind of music.

Carter's "American Period"

Attended by many influential commentators on new music, the Rome performance of the String Quartet No. 1, as David Schiff notes, "immediately established Carter's European reputation" and in effect "put Carter on the [worldwide] musical map."[3]

Carter's new European reputation as a composer of music characterized by "exceptionally virile writing" and by "strength and grandeur" in essence was not much different from his American reputation, in the making for at least a half-dozen years, as a creator of music that was "serious, complex, difficult, advanced[,] uncompromising," and "undeniably powerful."[4] Music of this sort, as Martin Boykan wrote in 1964, was "electrifying to [America's] postwar generation" and "spoke, in fact, for the America of the Fifties."[5] Yet it seems to have been even more electrifying and to have spoken its message more clearly to European audiences.

Schiff makes the cogent point that for some critics today Carter's 1951 String Quartet No. 1 and 1953–55 Variations for Orchestra—the work that occupied most of Carter's energies during his sojourn in Rome—rank among "the greatest American music of the 1950s," but he notes that during the 1950s these pieces in the United States "were little played, despite appreciative reviews and excellent recordings by the Walden Quartet and the Louisville Orchestra." Carter's status in his native country would soon change markedly, at least in part as a result of his being awarded a Pulitzer Prize for his 1959 String Quartet No. 2. Indeed, because all but one of the compositions that Carter produced in the two decades that encompass the String Quartet No. 2 and the 1980 *Night Fantasies* for solo piano were written specifically for American ensembles or solo performers, these years might well be termed, Schiff suggests, Carter's "American period."[6]

Commissions and promises of first performances during the 1960s and 1970s indeed came almost entirely from the Western Hemisphere. Nevertheless, Carter throughout these years was well aware of the obvious "contrast in reception [of his music] on the two sides of the Atlantic."[7] As a result, throughout his "American period" Carter opted to spend much of his time—including time devoted intensively to composition—in Europe.

Although the terms of his Prix de Rome allowed him to hold the residency for as long as three years, Carter opted to stay for just one, in large part because the limited cash allowance he received from the American Academy "did not even cover the rent" of the apartment in which he and his wife had chosen to live, "not to mention the cost of [tuition at] the American school for my son."[8] Carter returned to the United States in the late spring of 1954, but not before he had been elected vice president of the International Society for Contemporary Music (ISCM), and not before he had formed a close friendship with William Glock.

Eventually one of Carter's strongest European champions, Glock had been a music journalist for London's *Observer* from 1934 until 1945, when he was fired for penning a lengthy tribute to Béla Bartók instead of covering his assigned concerts. Hardly dissuaded, he immediately found work as a freelance critic; more significant, in 1948 he founded what eventually came to be known as the Dartington Summer Music School, in 1949 launched a journal called the *Score*, in 1954 was elected chair of the music division of the London-based Institute of Contemporary Arts (ICA), and in the same year began working as a consultant for the British Broadcasting Corporation.[9] All these activities had Glock heavily invested in the promotion of contemporary music; as a direct result of Glock's enthusiastic response to the Rome premiere of Carter's String Quartet No. 1, in 1955 not only did an article by Carter appear in the *Score*, but his music was featured at Dartington, on the ICA concert series, and—importantly—on BBC Radio.[10]

Carter was not able to attend the performances of his Cello Sonata and String Quartet No. 1 at Dartington during the summer of 1955. That summer he did, however, travel to Rome in order to attend meetings of the ISCM, and later he spent time at the ISCM festival at Baden-Baden. Vis-à-vis Carter's burgeoning international career, the visit to Baden-Baden was important not so much because it allowed Carter to hear yet another performance of the Cello Sonata but because it brought him into contact with Pierre Boulez, the French composer/conductor who, like Glock, would soon emerge as one of Carter's leading supporters in Europe.

In the fall of 1955 Carter accepted an appointment at Queens College in New York; he held the post for just one year and did not take on teaching duties again, at Yale, until 1960. Carter enjoyed the role of professor, but as had been the case several times before—when he served on the faculties at St. John's College from 1940 to 1942, at the Peabody Conservatory from 1946 to 1948, and at Columbia University from 1948 to 1950—he quickly realized that his wholehearted involvement with students demanded both time and energy that might be better spent, he felt, on composing.[11]

Significantly, by this time Carter—in terms of personal finances—was in a much better position to quit the working world and devote himself entirely to the production of music. This is not because Carter was suddenly besieged with commissions; after the Louisville Orchestra's generously funded request for the Variations for Orchestra, Carter's only other commission during this decade would be for the much-lauded String Quartet No. 2.[12] Nor was Carter's suddenly "secure" position due to the accelerating popularity of his music in European venues; performances both live and broadcast indeed generated revenue for Carter, but the income was hardly enough to support a family. Rather, Carter's newfound financial independence resulted from the simple fact that in April 1955 his father died. His late father's will granted to the composer a fairly large number of real-estate holdings in the New York City area; instead of retaining and managing these various properties, Carter opted to sell them.

Although Carter turned down an offer to teach at the 1956 Dartington Summer School, it seems likely that he was in attendance. He certainly participated in the Dartington event in 1957, teaching a two-week class in music analysis, hearing a performance of his Piano Sonata, and giving lectures on Stravinsky's ballet *Agon* and Schoenberg's Variations for Orchestra. In October 1957 Carter attended Germany's Donaueschingen Festival of Contemporary Music to witness a performance of his own Variations for Orchestra; later that month he was in Paris for a concert, sponsored by the U.S. Information Service, that featured the Parrenin Quartet reprising his now quite famous String Quartet No. 1.

In the late summer of 1958 Carter participated as a teacher in the Salzburg Seminars in American Studies.[13] Early in January 1959 the Italian Radio Orchestra gave a broadcast performance of his Variations for Orchestra; had he known about this soon enough in advance, Carter explained to the Italian composer Goffredo Petrassi, he happily would have gone to Rome for the occasion.[14] In the summer of 1959, after "coming back to earth" upon the completion of the String Quartet No. 2, Carter did travel again to Rome, in part to attend the seven-day ISCM festival but mostly to enjoy a five-week holiday.[15] He returned to the United States in mid-July, but later that year he was attending concerts and opera performances in Germany. To judge from various of his contemporaneous writings, Carter at around this time was proud of his identity as an American composer whose music was finding an audience abroad.[16] Yet both late in 1959 and early in 1960 he declined invitations from the U.S. State Department to represent American music on tours of countries behind the so-called iron curtain.[17]

In the fall of 1960, after his attendance at the ISCM festival in Cologne, Carter settled into yet another faculty position, this time at Yale. As had been the case with his earlier academic appointments, teaching for Carter proved enormously rewarding yet very much consuming of both the time and energy he wanted to spend on composing. The stint at Yale lasted just two years, after which Carter—following a visit as "invited guest" to the Warsaw Autumn Festival in September

1962—worked intensively on his Piano Concerto during a yearlong residency at the American Academy in Rome.

The Eternal City, clearly, had charms. As the composer later recalled: "[I] have returned there to the American Academy each time I planned to write a large work . . . for there I have been able to concentrate for long periods and have had the great pleasure of seeing my Italian friends and visiting the art in Rome that I love."[18] The Piano Concerto, completed for the most part in 1964, when Carter spent the year in Berlin under the auspices of the Ford Foundation and the Berlin government, certainly took shape in Rome during the 1962–63 residency; a stay at the American Academy in 1968–69 resulted in the completion of Carter's Concerto for Orchestra, and the *Night Fantasies* for solo piano—the last of the works from what Schiff calls Carter's "American period"—was brought to fruition there during a residency in 1979–80.

A "More Significant Temporal Thought"

The String Quartet No. 2 was composed not in Rome but in Waccabuc, New York, a small town about forty miles north of Manhattan where since 1952 Carter had maintained a lakeside residence. Even more than the three seminal works discussed in the previous chapter, this second string quartet counts as an important milestone in Carter's career. Whereas critics today still argue about which of those earlier works marks the precise point at which Carter's music began to sound distinctly "Carteresque," Carter himself has long been of the opinion that "his truly representative works only began with the Second Quartet."[19]

Aside from rhythmic complexities that exceeded any that Carter had produced thus far, what, one might wonder, was so special—or so different—about the 1959 String Quartet No. 2? What is it about the second quartet that not only separates it from all of Carter's previous efforts but also links it with practically all that came next?

As Schiff notes of the five string quartets that Carter produced between 1951 and 1996, it is the second that likely strikes listeners as "the most classical . . . because of its concision, formal clarity, and relative lightness of texture"; however much audiences might read in program notes about the work's allusions to twentieth-century modernist literature, the music they *hear* in Carter's second quartet "has the elegance and warmth of a Mozart quartet."[20] This may be so, but certainly not all of Carter's post-1959 music is remarkable for its lightness and warmth. And in terms of formal design, Carter by the late 1950s was hardly the neoclassicist that earlier—during and shortly after his studies with Boulanger—he might once have been.

Concision of form and clarity of expression may indeed be readily apparent hallmarks of the String Quartet No. 2, but there is more than that to this first of what the composer himself considers to be his "truly representative works." At least as Carter saw it, the breakthrough represented by the String Quartet No. 2—and by the more or less simultaneously composed Double Concerto for Piano and Harpsichord—had to do with an entirely new approach to what he called "musical time."

While one might quibble with Carter's statement that his compositional efforts had been directed toward music's "time dimension . . . since about 1940," few would contest the idea that he had been involved with explorations of the time dimension at least since the middle of that decade.[21] As daring as they were, however, Carter's experiments with musical time before 1957 had involved only quick yet measured shifts from one tempo to another and occasional moments in which two or more rates of flow occurred simultaneously. For all that Carter had to say about the first quartet being inspired by a Cocteau film in which real-time action, in effect, is contained within the opening and closing portions of a slow-motion frame, movement in this piece is for the most part linear, with one sonic "event" clearly coming after another. The moments in which Carter, in these earlier works, actually *plays* with time—or explores the concept of time itself—are in fact few and far between.

The possibilities of a radically new way of dealing with time, Carter later wrote, had occupied his thoughts throughout the 1950s, throughout the period, in other words, during which his international reputation was being solidly established not just with the 1951 String Quartet No. 1 but also with the 1953–55 Variations for Orchestra and, to a lesser extent, with the 1952 Sonata for Flute, Oboe, Cello, and Harpsichord and such earlier works as the 1945–46 Piano Sonata and the 1948 Sonata for Cello and Piano. And it is likely that his thoughts were furthered by what he heard as he made the rounds of the various European festivals devoted to contemporary music.

Asked if his "breakthrough" String Quartet No. 2 and Double Concerto were in some way reactions to European music of the sort regularly featured at the International Music Institute Darmstadt (IMD) festival, Carter said that at the time he felt that these were simply natural outgrowths of his first quartet, but he added that in retrospect he could see that they were at least in part "a response to the European avant-garde" as represented most famously by the works of his contemporary Olivier Messiaen and the younger composers Karlheinz Stockhausen and Pierre Boulez.[22] Although Carter was appreciative of certain ways in which these composers handled matters of pitch, he was generally dismissive of their formulaic treatment of musical time.

Recalling in particular his reactions to time-related issues in the music of Messiaen, Carter in 1990 remarked: "It's interesting to me that my First String Quartet was written almost exactly at the same time as those piano etudes of Messiaen that do all sorts of experimental things with rhythm. Evidently, Messiaen was thinking about the problem of how to deal with rhythm almost at the same period that I was."[23] Carter remarked further that the French composer in his experiments with rhythm, especially as evidenced in the "Mode de valeurs et d'intensités" (the third movement of the 1949 *Quatre études de rhythme* for solo piano), not only ended up taking a point of view very different from Carter's own but also produced results that, in Carter's view, were entirely unsatisfactory.

Granting that Messiaen's tightly organized treatment of volume levels and note durations in "Mode de valeurs et d'intensités" had significant impact on composers who eventually sought to apply serial methods to virtually all musical parameters, Carter said that, to his ears, the piece was "*very* unconvincing musically." To Carter, the very idea of serializing rhythmic values seemed "arbitrary" and "pointless," and the musical results—however meticulously realized by Messiaen or anyone else—typically sounded "very jerky."[24]

In terms of rhythm and time in general, Carter said, the essential difference between his own efforts and those of the leading European avant-garde composers was largely attitudinal. As Carter saw it, the serialism-dominated European cohort was likely hampered by the fact that it "had in its background a philosophy that . . . music should be *static*, with no sense of progression." In contrast, Carter said, his decidedly non-European, nonserial music involved the discovery of "*new* types of movement, changing from one speed to another, progressing from one kind of harmony to another."[25] Adventurous though it might have been in terms of pitch organization, Carter said, in temporal matters the "old-fashioned avant-gardism" of Stockhausen, Boulez, and others was "as routined as the regimens of the patients in Thomas Mann's *The Magic Mountain*."[26]

Well aware of what was transpiring in current European music and determined that in matters of musical time his own work should not at all be similarly "routined," Carter began a rigorous project that led directly to his String Quartet No. 2 and the Double Concerto. It was "an effort," Carter recalled, to explore through music a "more significant temporal thought."[27]

As noted earlier, one of Carter's professors at Harvard had been Alfred North Whitehead, a physicist/mathematician/philosopher who throughout his academic career pondered the nature of time and how time, in various ways, is understood by human beings. There is no telling how Carter initially might have been struck by Whitehead's famous notion that "what we perceive as the present is the vivid fringe of memory tinged with anticipation."[28] Carter at Harvard, after all, was still a young man, equipped only with a limited past and doubtless looking forward, as most young adults do, to a seemingly unlimited future. But by the time he completed the String Quartet No. 2 Carter was already fifty years old; what he might have anticipated at his personal half-century mark is anyone's guess, but surely by this point in his life Carter possessed enough of a past to bolster his "vivid fringe of memory" with substance aplenty.

It is clear that Carter, not just while his landmark String Quartet No. 2 was in progress but for years afterward, invested considerable intellectual energy into contemplating the relationships between the perceivable present and a blend of memories of the past with anticipations of the future. Specifically, Carter—during the production of the second quartet and other of his "truly representative" mature works—thought about how any individual's apparently objective grasp of the present is likely colored as much by subjective recollections of a real or imagined past as by projections (certainly subjective, possibly quite fantastic) of one or more possible futures. And on such "timely" concerns Carter articulated his thoughts on at least four occasions.

The least known—and earliest—of these is a lecture titled "Sound and Silence in Time: A Contemporary Approach to the Elements of Music" that was delivered on 13 February 1957 at the University of California, Los Angeles, during a three-day Carter fête that included performances of the Piano Sonata, the Variations for Orchestra, and the String Quartet No. 1.[29] More familiar, because each of them has been twice anthologized, are a brief 1965 lecture-based essay titled "The Time Dimension in Music" and a 1976 book chapter titled "Music and the Time Screen."[30] In addition, there is the 1965 "Time Lecture" that Carter delivered at Harvard.[31]

Summarizing the three last-mentioned of these, Jonathan W. Bernard notes that Carter's mature sense of time was likely influenced by such philosophical writings as Charles Koechlin's 1926 essay "Le temps et la musique," Pierre Suvchinsky's 1939 article "La notion du temps et la musique," and Gisèle Brelet's two-volume 1949 *Le temps musical: Essai d'une esthétique nouvelle de la musique.*[32]

Although it remains unclear whether or not these texts were known to Carter when they were first published, they are certainly cited in both Carter's "Music and the Time Screen" chapter and his "Time Lecture." But Carter, in his various efforts to explain his new "temporal thought," also deals with ideas about time as expressed by serious thinkers who range chronologically from Greek antiquity (Plato and Pythagoras, explicitly, but by implication also Aristoxenus) through the heyday of music's "common practice period" (Hegel, explicitly, but by implication also Kant and Hanslick) to the time of his own writings; the more or less contemporaneous thinkers he cites include Henri Bergson, Edmund Husserl, Martin Heidegger, and Susanne K. Langer.

"Music and the Time Screen" is the longest of Carter's formal discourses on time; fitted with six excerpts from published scores and two charts that illustrate pitch sets used in the Concerto for Orchestra, it is also the one in which Carter deals most extensively with his own music. Regarding questions of time explored through music, this 1976 book chapter counts as Carter's most technical text, yet the most theoretical discussion of the subject of time seems to be the lecture that Carter gave at UCLA almost two decades earlier. Indeed, in their introduction to the 1957 "Sound and Silence in Time," Felix Meyer and Anne C. Shreffler suggest that this lecture, which deals with "the most basic elements of music and their psychological and physiological implications," is the "most theoretical text" that Carter produced on *any* subject.[33]

Meyer and Shreffler rather boldly state that "it is hard to avoid the conclusion that Carter's extensive ruminations on silence must have had something to do with his encounter" with the recordings of the complete works of Anton Webern that had been released earlier in 1957. There is documentary evidence to support the idea that Carter at around this time listened to and was intrigued by the Webern recordings. But one might just as well suppose that Carter's ruminations had at least something to do with the public celebrations of "silence" that throughout the 1950s had been conducted—with much publicity and controversy—by Carter's compatriot John Cage. In any case, the only composers that Carter in fact mentions during his "Sound and Silence in Time" lecture are Mozart, Wagner, Debussy, Schoenberg, Stravinsky, and Bruno Maderna. But the important gist of Carter's "Sound and Silence in Time" has little to do with music by any composer or even with music per se; ultimately, the lecture concerns human beings' various perceptions of time.

Aptly alluding to the cinema, an art form that had come of age during Carter's early adulthood and whose Hollywood-based norms in the postwar years were fairly endemic, Carter told his audience:

> As our lives are projected in this moving picture of eternity, we gain a very rich experience of the passage of time; our first breath starts sometimes with a slap like the attack of an instrument, and our organic clock begins ticking and beating, at the same time drawing a history of itself like a cardiogram on our memories. And then there are the vast number of things we learn, forget, dimly remember, experience, enjoy, compare, think about—all of them operating the most remarkable tricks with time. We learn about thousands of years in a few seconds and about some remarkable thing that took but a few minutes by thinking about it for many hours.[34]

At several points in the course of the lecture Carter touches on the phenomenon that later he would call simply "musical time" but that in his first disquisition on the subject he designates not only by that term but also by such formulations as "design in time," "temporal order," "abstract activity in time," "the inner experience of time," and the "experience of time [that] music articulates." Carter never comes right out and declares it, but one suspects that he realized full well that this "most unique and valuable" experience lent itself to articulation much more easily through music than through words.[35] Tellingly, Carter in this lecture never gives a clear definition of the "musical time" that is his central topic. Instead, he likens it to what transpires when an intelligent person encounters an essay's written language:

> Each successive word gives a more precise meaning to the one or ones that have gone before. A word, at first vague, is modified, then its signification given perhaps a location in time and space. Sentence after sentence it continues to change and mold the meaning. Sentence modifies sentence and paragraph modifies paragraph. Whole large subjects are contrasted with others—[readers'] objections are considered, there is an ever widening context which can all be made to throw light on the basic ideas.[36]

The same thing occurs in music, Carter says, the essential difference being that combinations of musical tones in most cases "refer" neither to things nor to ideas but only to themselves. Using imagery that was shared by a large number of university-based American musicologists, music theorists, and composers who in the postwar years championed the idea of "autonomous" music, Carter concludes his analogy by explaining that "the interconnection of tones" in music—unlike the syntactical linkages between words in a written essay—is a matter of "the combination of many kinds of tensions [that are] interpreted by the listener as a web of cause and effect, of effort, energy, satisfaction, relaxation." What transpires in any well-made piece of music, Carter offers, is in effect "a series of remarkably motivated happenings"; to a certain extent these "happenings" might seem fully "expected," Carter says, yet "when they really make their appearance [they seem] always surprising and novel."[37]

Despite his solid grounding in Whitehead-based philosophy and his obvious knack for translating abstract musical ideas into lucid prose, Carter in his later writings continued to dance around the question of what, precisely, is meant by the term "musical time." The primary purpose of his 1976 "Music and the Time Screen," Carter announces near the beginning of the book chapter, is to describe how he, "out of a consideration for the special temporality of music, [has] attempted to derive a way of composing that deals with [the] very nature" of time. But before he can do that, he writes, he must first deal with the idea of time itself. It is a "formidable subject" and "a most confusing one," he admits, "because no common vocabulary exists to help us."[38]

To give readers a sample of the multiple time-related vocabularies available to the modern thinker, Carter had included in his 1965 "Time Lecture" fairly complete definitions not just of the ancient Greek notions of *aiōn* ("a long period of time"), *kairos* ("the critical moment for action"), and *khronos* ("a certain definite stretch of time, such as a season") but also of Brelet's *temps pathologique* ("subjective" or "passive" time) as opposed to both *temps empirique* ("objective, active, or empirical time") and *temps vécu* ("experienced time").[39] Carter omits these in his 1976 "Music and the Time Screen," but to make the same point he begins by quoting Koechlin's definitions of four "aspects of time" ("pure duration," "psychological time," "mathematically measured time," and "musical time") and then briefly compares these terms—and the concepts behind them—with Bergson's "real" or "subjective" time (*la durée réelle*), Heidegger's "public time," Suvchinsky's "chronometric time," Husserl's "stream of lived experience" and "internal time-consciousness," and Langer's "clock time," "virtual time," and "sense of transience."[40]

Some of these terms are practically synonymous, Carter suggests, while others—although they rely on similar words—are diametrically opposed in meaning. For help in clarification, Carter draws on Langer's 1953 *Feeling and Form*, a book that for him "has been illuminating on these matters."[41] Indeed, on four occasions Carter quotes directly from the chapter that Langer titles "The Image of Time." The first quotation to an extent supports Carter's opening claim that the topic of time in general has perennially been difficult; more significant, it leads toward the one aspect of time that Carter, as a composer, finds most intriguing: "Every conceptual form which is supposed to portray time oversimplifies it to the point of leaving out the most interesting aspects of it, namely the characteristic appearance of passage."[42]

The next two quotations from Langer articulate the difference, which, Carter suggests, should be obvious to anyone of normal intelligence, between time as it might be measured by a ticking clock and time as it might be *felt* by a particular person in a particular situation. The fourth and longest quotation follows Carter's own explication of musical time. Condensed by Carter into just two paragraphs fitted with ellipses, in Langer the material comprises three paragraphs that cover almost two full pages and whose footnotes, as does Carter's text, make reference to Koechlin, Husserl, and Heidegger. Like the first quotation, this last one concludes with a pithy sentence that in effect summarizes Carter's thoughts on musical time:

> The underlying principle of clock-time is *change,* which is measured by contrasting two states of an instrument, whether that instrument be the sun in various positions, or the hand on a dial at successive locations, or a parade of monotonous, similar events like ticks or flashes, "counted," i.e., differentiated, by being correlated with a series of distinct numbers. . . ."Change" is not itself something presented; it is implicitly given through the contrast of different "states," themselves unchanging.
>
> The time-concept which emerges from such mensuration is something far removed from time as we know it in direct experience, which is essentially *passage,* or the sense of transience. . . . But the experience of time is anything but simple. It involves more properties than "length," or interval between selected moments; for its passages have also what I can only call, metaphorically, *volume.* Subjectively, a unit of time may be great or small as well as long or short. . . . It is this voluminousness of the direct experience of passage that makes it . . . indivisible. But even its volume is not simple; for it is filled with its own characteristic forms, as space is filled with material forms, otherwise it could not be observed and appreciated. . . . The primary illusion of music is the sonorous image of passage, abstracted from actuality to become free and plastic, and entirely perceptible.[43]

The possibility of a "sonorous image" of the passage of subjective time—an image perhaps illusory but nevertheless an image that makes the *sense* of passage "entirely perceptible" to the listener—seems to have been at the very heart of the thinking that for Carter began with his work on the 1959 String Quartet No. 2. More to the point, meticulous realizations of sonic imagery that somehow depicts the subjective "experience of passage" are at the very heart of Carter's mature music.

Carter declared as much in the two lectures that preceded "Music and the Time Screen" by eleven years. In 1965, near the beginning of "The Time Dimension in Music," he said that his work had long been focused on various perceptions of time and that whatever innovative compositional techniques he had used were "contributory to the main concern of dealing with our experience of time, [with] trying to communicate my own experience of it and my awareness of this experience in others."[44] Also in 1965, near the end of his "Time Lecture," Carter said that in his music, as in life in general, "any given moment, for the most part, is a bridge from a previous one to a succeeding one and contains both the elements of unexpectedness as well as intelligible relation to the past and anticipation of the future, not always fulfilled in the way anticipated." Significantly, Carter told the Harvard audience that it is this idea—bolstered by an awareness of how "even small details [can] participate in larger constructions" and contribute to a work's "large continuity and conception of progress"—that "determines the choice of *all* the materials in my recent work."[45]

"Local Details" and "Dramatic Development"

His recent work differed in many ways from that of his contemporaries, Carter told an interviewer in 1969, but perhaps the most striking difference had to do with treatments of musical "instants." Generalizing sweepingly, Carter said that for the most part European and American postwar modernists had been "very routine" in the way they handled "any given instant of music," and "usually they settled for harmonic effects that emphasize certain qualities of the theme, or contrapuntal ones that repeat fragments of the main theme in order, so to speak, to cook the chicken in chicken broth, to intensify its particular character." In contrast, his own music invariably treated instants not as singular moments in a linear progression of ideas but as fragments of an always imaginable whole. "I was interested in flow," Carter said, "in the contribution of the past to the present and the effect of predicted futures on it, in dealing with the process of an emerging present."[46]

This is a heady statement, and it raises again the questions posed early in the preceding section of this chapter. To summarize rather bluntly, quite aside from all that Carter had to say about his "more significant temporal thought," how—in sound and in positivistic musical fact—does the String Quartet No. 2 really differ from Carter's earlier music?

One immediately apparent characteristic of Carter's mature music is its relatively enormous amount of time-related information. Carter's earlier works that addressed matters of time are remarkable both for their metric modulations and for their overlays of tempos. These two basic devices—the one involving different rates of musical flow presented in succession, the other involving different rates of flow presented simultaneously—are evident in all of Carter's music beginning with the Piano Sonata, and they certainly figure into the String Quartet No. 2 and what followed. But whereas in the earlier works these techniques were used primarily at a composition's arguably "special" moments, in the later works they are pervasive. Beginning with the String Quartet No. 2, there are almost no special moments at which a listener's attention will be drawn to a single temporal activity; instead, the many moments of these later compositions tend to be always filled with multiple and often seemingly contradictory temporal activities.

A second distinctive characteristic of Carter's mature music is perhaps less apparent to the ear but is nevertheless crucially related to the listening experience. Indeed, it is this second characteristic that makes possible the first characteristic's perception.

Regarded in isolation (i.e., separated from the composition as a whole and considered only as single strands of a large musical fabric), the individual temporal activities of Carter's mature compositions in most cases seem logically enough related to what comes before and after; regarded as they actually occur (i.e., simultaneous with any number of other activities), the individual activities have the potential to be heard only as components of a sonic blur. If collectively they are *not* perceived as a blur, it is because Carter gives each of them a sharply defined identity. Not only is each line of thought governed by a logic all its own, but each strand of the musical fabric is associated with a unique set of timbres, rhythmic gestures, dynamic shapes, and—especially important in the later, larger works—pitch structures and spatial elements.

Thus a potentially clarifying light is shed on even the densest passages. And thus the average willing and attentive listener, while likely not able to follow all of what transpires at any given moment, nevertheless gets the impression that what transpires is not at all a mere jumble; the impression made by Carter's mature music, rather, is that of a multiplicity of discrete ideas that seem at least somehow sensible in their collective entirety.

As he worked on his two style-defining pieces Carter sought answers to several questions that for him were especially bothersome. "How [should] events [be] presented, carried on, and accompanied?" he asked himself. "What kind of changes can previously presented events undergo while maintaining some element of identity? And how can all this be used to express compelling aspects of experience to the listener?"[47] The second and third of these questions are of a philosophical nature and thus lend themselves to vague responses. In contrast, the first question, pertaining only to the ways in which different "events" might be presented, in Carter's music found concrete answers.

Whereas the essential problem of the String Quartet No. 2, as Carter explained, was "to differentiate instruments of similar character," the essential problem of the Double Concerto "was to join together instruments of very different basic characteristics."[48] In both works—and in such later pieces as the 1965 Piano Concerto, the 1974 Duo for Violin and Piano, and the 1976 Symphony of Three Orchestras—Carter's solutions to these problems in part involved suggestions or instructions for the onstage array of the participating performers. In the string quartet, for example, he asked only that the players sit farther apart than usual; for the Double Concerto, he drew up an elaborate seating plan that positioned not just the two solo instruments but also the members of their widely spaced accompanying chamber orchestras.

But a more significant way in which Carter dealt with the problem of presentation of musical events—doubtless useful to keen-eared listeners who might experience this music not "live" in the three-dimensional space of a concert hall but via a monophonic recording—involved assigning to the various musical protagonists distinct yet ultimately compatible pitch- and rhythm-based materials. Carter explained that in the Double Concerto, for example, the piano is assigned "the all-interval four-note chord, E–F–A-flat–B-flat, but spaced according to the intervals that are connected with the piano, while the other all-interval chord of E–F–G–B, which is in the harpsichord, is spaced according to the intervals that are used in the harpsichord."[49] Indeed, Carter said, the differentiation of forces in the Double Concerto depends crucially not so much on specific pitches but "on the sound of intervals, combined with various tone colors."[50] As for the rhythmic content of the Double Concerto, one might say with accuracy, as Carter did, that it is simply a matter of "the speeding up and slowing down of themes."[51] But the rhythmic content also entails a meticulously planned set of tempos that "divide up the ratio of 2:1 according to two mathematical series" in order to produce "five speeds [that] are in a ratio of whole numbers—10:9:8:7:6:5—and five [that] are in a ratio of reciprocals—1/10:1/9:1/8:1/7:1/6:1/5."[52]

Mathematical relationships between the various speeds of the String Quartet No. 2 are not nearly so complex; here, too, contrasting rates of musical flow are brought into conflict with one another, but the four instruments are "stratified" not so much by tempo as by "their repertoire of intervals, their repertoire of rhythms, and their repertoire of musical gestures." Carter explained:

> The first violin, for example, specializes in the intervals of the minor third, the perfect fifth, major ninth, and major tenth. Its fantastic and ornate character is borne out by its rhythmic repertoire, which is extremely contrasted. The second violin, on the other hand, shows very regular motion and moves steadily at its own metronome markings of 140, 70, and sometimes 280. The viola specializes in rhythmic relationships which are usually in the ratio 2:3 or 3:5, and the cello does not move at a steady tempo, but rather has accelerandos and ritards built in. This stratification of the instruments can be heard very clearly at the begin-

ning of the piece. As the piece progresses, the diverse "characters" of the beginning come to influence each other and the repertoires of each "actor" begin to be shared.[53]

The last sentence of the just-quoted paragraph alludes to the most striking and the most readily perceptible way in which Carter in his "truly representative" compositions managed the presentation of musical events.

That music should be fundamentally dramatic was of course an idea that Carter had explored since the mid-1940s, and this idea would sustain him for the rest of his career. As had been the case with the three seminal works discussed in the previous chapter, Carter in his mature works thought of various musical components as individual "actors" who, so that they might be easily recognized by an audience, needed to be not just distinctly "garbed" but also equipped with a "personality" whose elements—at least at the drama's start—are unique to them alone. Asked how he went about writing a new work, Carter once replied that he typically devised a precomposition plan that included such "local details" as rhythmic schemes, pitch content, and interval structures. But usually he began, he said, "with an idea of the sound, the musical character, and the dramatic development of these, similar to the plot—or subject—outline of a novel or play, or the scenario of a movie."[54]

One suspects that most sensitive lay listeners upon experiencing a Carter work would realize quite on their own that the music had dramatic qualities aplenty. Jonathan W. Bernard, in a 1988 summary of Carter's work, was obviously addressing a different audience when he observed that the clear fact that "beginning with the Second Quartet Carter conceives the larger design of each of his works according to some dramatic plan" is something "the *analyst* needs to know."[55]

Carter's music had been dramatic since the 1940s, but a major difference between the musical dramas offered by Carter's seminal works and those of his mature works has to do with the nature of the temporal planes on which the dramas are enacted.

The earlier works almost always treat time as though it were a simple linear continuum; they emulate classical-style Hollywood films, in which for the most part one depicted event follows another in an apparently logical real-time sequence and in which alterations of this pattern (realized often with the device known as a flashback, more rarely with an enactment of an imagined or hypothetical situation) count as something, in terms of traditional narrative design, extraordinary. In Carter's mature works, although a performance of course transpires over a span of chronological real time that usually begins with an authoritative downbeat and concludes with an impactful silence, time, at least as Carter conceived of it, often seems to be not so much linear as fluid.

Since Carter himself likened the typical dramatic plan for one of his compositions to "the scenario of a movie," it seems fruitful to mention here a few examples of cinema that demonstrate time-play of the sort that Carter attempted to verbalize in the writings and lectures cited above and that he articulated in countless ways in his music. Already mentioned in the previous chapter has been Carter's comparison of the cadenzas that open and close his 1951 String Quartet No. 1 with the slow-motion sequences that frame the normal-speed main content of Cocteau's 1930 *Le sang d'une poète*. Another cinematic model might be Akira Kurosawa's 1950 *Rashomon*.

The central idea of Kurosawa's film, so well known that the "*Rashomon* effect" is now a fashionable courtroom term, is that different individuals can participate in the same event yet account for it in drastically contrasting ways. Between fragments of a real-time narrative, *Rashomon* presents in succession four severely conflicting "eyewitness" accounts of a single incident. After the initial and seemingly credible telling of the story, the audience member is led to regard *all* the narrated information—what has already been presented, what is being presented at the moment, whatever might be presented in the future—with increasing skepticism. No mention of *Rashomon* is made in the anthologies of Carter's writing, and perhaps Carter in fact did not know the film. Nevertheless, *Rashomon* is likely to be in the mind of any cinephile who comes across Carter's description of his 1969 Concerto for Orchestra and its "four main characters," hints of which "are being referred to constantly" even as "one facet after another" is emphasized at the momentary expense of the others.[56]

A more apt cinematic model for what Carter sought to accomplish with nearly all his mature music is Alain Resnais' *Last Year at Marienbad*, a French film completed in the same year as Carter's Double Concerto. This is a film that Carter possibly knew, for in a 1965 essay he mentioned the author of its screenplay, Alain Robbe-Grillet, as one of the literary figures whose work has "encouraged musicians to find new ways of dealing with perception, recognition, understanding, experience, and memory."[57] In any case, the decidedly nonlinear and mostly conversational "action" of *Last Year at Marienbad* revolves around a man and a woman who may or may not have known each other in the past, who may or may not be correctly interpreting the present, who may or may not be dreaming or even hallucinating about the future.

In a 1961 article, Robbe-Grillet, in language that Carter surely would have appreciated, contrasted the time-warping nature of *Last Year at Marienbad* with the temporal flow of classical-style film:

> Everyone knows the linear plots of the old-fashioned cinema, which never spare us a link in the chain of all-too-expected events: the telephone rings, a man picks up the receiver, then we see the man who is on the other end of the line, the first man says he's coming, hangs up, walks out the door, down the stairs, gets into his car, drives through the streets, parks his car in front of a building, goes in, climbs the stairs, rings the bell, someone opens the door, etc. In reality, our mind goes faster—or slower, on occasion. Its style is more varied, richer, and less reassuring: it skips certain passages, it preserves an exact record of certain "unimportant" details, it repeats and doubles back on itself. And this *mental time,* with its peculiarities, its gaps, its obsessions, its obscure areas, is the one that interests us, since it is the tempo of our emotions, of our *life.*[58]

In language that Carter perhaps would have agreed with but nevertheless likely would have taken as a challenge, Robbe-Grillet attested that there can be no doubt that "cinema is the preordained means of expression for a story" in which memory, observation, speculation, and the like are mixed fluidly together. After all, Robbe-Grillet wrote, "the essential characteristic of the [on-screen filmic] image" is that, no matter what it might suggest about a fictional past or future, its content inevitably transpires in the present before the viewers' eyes. Quite unlike written literature, which "has a whole gamut of grammatical tenses that makes it possible to narrate events in relation to each other," the cinema—because of the nature of the medium—in effect offers verbs only "in the present tense." Thus, Robbe-Grillet concluded, what the cinema audience sees and hears is always "in the act of happening"; always, the audience is "given the gesture itself," not merely "an account of it."[59]

Robbe-Grillet is correct in suggesting that cinema, capable as it is of conveying information as much with imagery as with language, is particularly suitable to artists who might choose to work in nonlinear narrative modes. Yet most of what Robbe-Grillet says here can apply just as well to music, a medium whose units of information—although not nearly so explicit in content as those of language or imagery—are similarly absorbed by listeners in real time and whose "verbs," like those of cinema, seem to be always "in the present tense."

In his many comments that deal with comparisons of his own mature music with representative examples from Western art music's long-flowing mainstream, Carter has made it abundantly clear that the essential difference had to do with the various composers' conceptions and attempted realizations of what he called "musical" time. Not disparagingly but appreciatively, Carter acknowledged that the great bulk of post-Enlightenment Western music progresses logically and often quite beautifully according to what Robbe-Grillet, referring to the bulk of cinema, called "some 'Cartesian' schema."[60] Yet Carter was especially drawn to those relatively few examples of post-Enlightenment music in which the governing schema seems not so much "Cartesian" as "Carterian."

Considering the dramatic nature of his own music, it is hardly surprising that the passages that Carter cites as possible models come not from the repertoire of the concert hall but from the repertoire of opera. For early instances of "simultaneously interacting heterogeneous character-continuities" and the "simultaneous interaction of a number of very different musical sub-continuities" of the sort that characterize his mature music, Carter points to operatic scenes in which several characters with quite different agendas hold forth onstage at the same time. Specific excerpts that Carter mentions include the ballroom scene in Mozart's *Don Giovanni*, the finale of the second act of Verdi's *Falstaff*, and the finale of the same composer's *Aida*.[61]

In his 1970 liner note for a recording of his String Quartet No. 2, Carter described the four instruments as being "to a certain extent . . . type-cast," with each of them functioning "in a certain sense . . . like a character in an opera made up primarily of 'quartets.'"[62] In his 1976 "Music and the Time Screen," he surveyed everything he had composed since the second quartet and to a certain extent projected his future course; Carter observed that his "truly representative" compositions—those already composed and, presumably, those yet to come—depend on

> a special dimension of time, that of "multiple perspective," in which various contrasting characters are presented simultaneously. . . . Double and sometimes manifold character simultaneities, of course, present, as our human experience often does, certain emotionally charged events as seen in the context of others, producing often a kind of irony, which I am particularly interested in. In doing this so frequently, and by leading into and away from such moments in what seemed to me telling ways, I have, I think, been trying to make moments of music as rich in reference as I could.[63]

Perhaps momentarily forgetting the films of Cocteau and Eisenstein that apparently influenced him in the late 1920s as well as the novels of Robbe-Grillet and others that he felt had led postwar composers toward adventurously new ways of thinking about time, Carter exaggerates when he writes that the simultaneous presentation of multiple perspectives is "something that can be done *only* in music." But Carter is quite on the mark when he notes that within music's limited arena such a presentation, before his 1957 String Quartet No. 2, had "rarely been achieved except in opera."[64]

Assessment

Carter decided in the late 1950s to explore to the fullest not just the momentary effects of metric modulation and tempo superimpositions but also the almost constant presentation of multiple strands of musical thought. This was a bold move, and it came not without a certain cost. Now the "subject" of all his music, time—in the literal sense—was something that Carter needed to invest into his work all the more heavily.

"In choosing the path he did," writes Bernard, "Carter had certainly not made things easier for himself. As the 1950s gave way to the 1960s, his compositions were taking longer and longer to complete: the Piano Concerto (1965) and the Concerto for Orchestra (1969) were each the product of four years of effort."[65] The Piano Concerto and the Concerto for Orchestra indeed represent one temporal extreme of Carter's new modus operandi. But in fact most of Carter's other mature works—the 1959 String Quartet No. 2, the 1961 Double Concerto, the 1971 String Quartet No. 3, the 1974 Duo for Violin and Piano, the 1974 Brass Quintet, the 1975 *A Mirror on Which to Dwell* (a setting for soprano and chamber ensemble of six poems by Elizabeth Bishop), the 1976 Symphony of Three Orchestras, the 1978 *Syringa* (settings for mezzo-soprano, baritone, and chamber ensemble of poems by John Ashbery), the 1980 *Night Fantasies* for solo piano—took only a year or so, and sometimes less, to complete.

So far as timetables are concerned, perhaps all that really matters is the "average" amount of chronological time Carter spent on the meticulous writing of his time-oriented mature works measured against the "average" reception of these works by influential performers and critics. Surveying a span of three decades, Meyer and Shreffler note that between 1950 and 1980 "Carter composed only thirteen major works."[66] The production of a mere thirteen "major" works over a thirty-year period of almost full-time compositional activity might seem at first glance to be rather unimpressive. It should be noted, though, that Carter proceeded along his chosen path not just slowly but also surely. As a result, not because of the length of time required of the individual works but because of the skill with which the works were made, Carter during his "American period" developed an international reputation as a reliable producer of musical masterpieces.

In 1973, reviewing the premiere performance of the String Quartet No. 3 (the second work for which Carter won the prestigious Pulitzer Prize for Music), Andrew Porter offered that "Elliott Carter . . . is now America's most famous living composer." Perhaps because he was still adjusting to his position as an Englishman recently engaged as music critic for the *New Yorker*, Porter emphasized Carter's qualities as an "American" composer:

> He unites two qualities that, particularly in their combination, strike a European as especially American: a breadth and range of cultural experience (not only musical), evinced in his education, his writings, and his compositions, that can make many otherwise comparable European creators seem nationalistic, even local, and a "ruggedness" of artistic temperament, a heroism most conveniently termed Ivesian, which, when all the worlds of music lie known and open to him, leads him to choose and pursue his own unfaltering path—not blinkered but with a full, commanding view over the paths that others are taking.[67]

Six years later Porter assessed Carter from a broader perspective. Prompted immediately by the premiere of *Syringa* but contemplating a number of Carter performances mounted to celebrate the composer's seventieth birthday, Porter wrote: "In a 'world view' there are perhaps six established very important composers active today: Carter and Tippett, now in their seventies; Boulez, Henze, and Stockhausen, in their fifties; and Maxwell Davies, in his forties. . . . Any attempt to order the six would be silly; each of them has different things to offer, on which various listeners place different values. But I think it at least likely that if there were to be an international poll to nominate 'the greatest living composer,' Carter's name would lead all the rest."[68]

Virgil Thomson, whose review of the Piano Sonata had done much to further Carter's career, early in his 1971 *American Music since 1910* called Carter one of those rare American artists who, like writer Edgar Allan Poe and fellow composer Carl Ruggles, "wear their integrity on their sleeve"; as with Ruggles, Thomson wrote, Carter's output to date was relatively small, "but no compromise has taken place, nor has any hindrance occurred to the artist's full ripening." Toward the end of the book, in a dictionary-like section that gives information on 106 American composers, Thomson expressed a more specific opinion. Although Thomson felt that Carter's orchestral works were generally "lacking in strength of line," in his opinion Carter's chamber music was "the most interesting being composed today by anybody anywhere. And I mean intrinsically interesting, not merely attractive to the ear. His genius is to have combined intellectual elaboration and auditory delight with no loss of intensity to either."[69]

Relating Carter to both Thomson and Aaron Copland, Irving Kolodin, longtime music critic for the *Saturday Review*, in the epilogue of his 1980 *In Quest of Music: A Journey in Time* dubbed Carter "a father figure" of contemporary American composers, someone who had "emerged from the climate of encouragement" in which Thomson and Copland had thrived and who eventually became the "fulfillment" of those composers' dreams. Carter, Kolodin wrote, "is a man whose intellectual vigor and aesthetic conscience are producing works which show no signs of diminution in interest at home, and ever increasing recognition abroad."[70]

These various assessments of Carter toward the end of his American period are certainly interesting, especially in the ways they attempt to measure Carter's position as an American composer against his position as an international composer. But, by and large, these and countless other, in effect, journalistic reports simply pass favorable judgment upon Carter; for the most part, they do not even attempt to explain *why* virtually all of Carter's compositions, beginning with the 1951 String Quartet No. 1 and extending at least over the next three decades, perhaps count as "great" music.

Surprisingly, considering how different in both content and intent from Carter's music his own music has always been, one of the clearest articulations of the reasons for Carter's status as an arguably "great" composer has come from Ned Rorem. Referring to their disparate approaches to such basic musical concepts as tonal center and rhythmic pulse, in 1980 the archly conservative Rorem suggested that the ultramodernist Carter "seems the farthest pole from me," yet he would probably agree that what both of them have "strived for most" is simplicity of expression.[71] Referring to even more fundamental concepts, Rorem six years earlier had written:

> Necessity is what Carter projects. Not, as some would have it, the necessity of intellect but the clean-cut necessity of a child's fit. Like never-resting souls tangled in hell proceed his bowed counterpoints, and always in performance after performance they are *tangled in the same way*, like those viscous strands on a [Jackson] Pollock canvas that, actually still, seem to move through time. Nothing great is ever left to chance, and great Carter surely is in his ability to notate insanity with a precision that, after the fifth or twelfth hearing, renders the notes as logical as the placement of beasts in the Peaceable Kingdom.[72]

"Greatness in music" is, of course, a slippery topic. Leonard B. Meyer, whose 1956 *Emotion and Meaning in Music* had examined many of the memory- and expectation- related issues that Carter discussed in his 1957 "Sound and Silence in Time" lecture, addressed the matter head-on in a 1959 essay titled "Some Remarks on Value and Greatness in Music." Meyer perhaps would have won

Carter's approval with his quotation from Norbert Wiener, founder of the then-popular field known as cybernetics and the still-popular field known as information theory, to the effect that in any circumstances a surfeit of fulfilled expectation makes for a dull experience. But Meyer's conclusion is that the only real criterion for greatness in music is a vague and transcendent expressive content that somehow poses to listeners the question: "What is the meaning and purpose of man's existence?"[73] Meyer admits that his prime criterion for musical greatness is ultimately metaphysical, and one of Meyer's strongest supporters points out that, according to this criterion, the "function" of great music is "essentially a religious one."[74] For such a conclusion Carter—always a rationalist at least in his public utterances—probably would not have had much use.

But Carter likely would have appreciated the rather different concept of "greatness in music" explored by Alfred Einstein in a 1941 book by that title. For Einstein, the admittedly elusive and perhaps ineffable quality of musical greatness had nothing at all to do with profound metaphysical questions or with historical impact, or with excellence in craftsmanship or with originality. Rather, "what distinguishes genius from talent"—in other words, what makes some music great—are such matters as "condensation" and "universality." Most important, for Einstein greatness in music entailed "the construction of an inner world, and the communication of this inner world to the physical world of humanity."[75]

The meticulous construction of various musical inner worlds and the relating of the many dramas, small and large, that transpire within those worlds is perhaps at the heart of Carter's mature music. Simply to establish a flow of musical oppositions takes no particular imagination. Nor is it especially difficult to bring at least a semblance of unity to sharply contrasting musical ideas; musically non-literate elementary-school students could do this on a moment's notice simply by deciding upon a limited vocabulary of sonic ingredients and then making sure that every one of their perhaps wildly improvised gestures holds to the "rule." But it requires skill, and a truly "musical" ear, to do this in a way that sounds at least reasonably interesting. And to do it in a way that is overwhelmingly effective—so that the listener is held on the edge of his chair for the duration of a performance and then dropped back, spent but satisfied—requires something more.

Elliott Carter's genius, consistently apparent in the works composed between 1950 and 1980, lies partly in the sheer emotive strength of his musical gestures, virtually all of which have an impact, no matter how many of them are being heard simultaneously. It lies partly, too, in the richness of his materials and partly in the subtlety with which he is able to conjure up sensual images of polarity while at the same time informing the listener's brain that the ostensibly disparate sounds are in fact intimately connected. Perhaps most of all, Carter's genius—apropos of the "more significant temporal thought" that governed this period of his career—lies in his acute sense of timing, his ability to place not just front-and-center musical ideas but also their foretastes and afterglows within a span of time in such a way that every sound seems, somehow, to have meaning and purpose.

4 New Directions (1980–2010)

BETWEEN 1950 AND 1980 virtually all of Elliott Carter's compositions were written for and premiered by American artists. Yet during these decades his music had plenty of performances in Europe, and Carter was of the general opinion that his works were not only better treated in terms of allotted rehearsal time but also better received, not just by the press but by audiences, in Europe than in his native country. It probably came as no great shock, then, that in April 1980 Carter was notified that he was soon to be granted the Ernst von Siemens Prize, a Munich-based award that had been established in 1972 and that has often been described—albeit not without some exaggeration—as the musical world's equivalent of the Nobel Prize.[1]

The official document accompanying the presentation of the Siemens Prize informed Carter that the honor was in recognition of his "meritorious achievements in the opening up of new musical directions, which, in works abounding with originality, have made him a leading composer of the present day."[2] In his acceptance speech Carter humbly thanked not just the many "excellent" and "committed" performers who over the previous decades had presented his own music in public but also the "long-suffering, patient audiences" who had "courageously listened to so many relatively uninteresting works of newly composed music in the hope of finding a few scores that made the trial worthwhile." Intriguingly,

Carter also expressed a debt of gratitude to humanity in general, or at least to "the human feelings and thoughts new music evokes that are only partially unique to their composer, being mainly made up of the experiences all of us have had living in this very turbulent century, trying to understand it, trying to find a way of living in the midst of its appalling problems and its over-publicized consumerist hedonism."[3]

The reference to "this very turbulent century" and "trying to find a way of living in the midst of its appalling problems" has deep undertones, for at the time of the acceptance speech Carter was at work on *In Sleep, in Thunder*, a setting of six verses by Robert Lowell, the American poet whose mind was quite nearly unraveled at the time of his death in 1977. As David Schiff points out, *In Sleep, in Thunder* is "one of Carter's most forbidding works," an "unmediated vision of the way we live now."[4]

Vis-à-vis Lowell, the musical treatment of poetry that is manic, desperate, and often violent is certainly biographical; whether or not the piece is to any extent autobiographical, vis-à-vis Carter, is open to debate. To be sure, Carter's published comments suggest that *In Sleep, in Thunder* for all its acidulousness is, in the composer's view, simply a piece of dramatic music. Yet Schiff, a Carter student who over the years has engaged his former teacher in many private conversations, hints strongly that the poems as arranged and set by Carter tell not just the particular story of Lowell's private hell "but also a generic [story] about the fate of the artist in America" and that with this composition "Carter takes on a persona to explore and exorcise his own feelings of isolation and anger." Indeed, the pervasive theme of the 1998 second edition of Schiff's *Music of Elliott Carter* seems to be that in the world of American music as it evolved since the early 1980s "Carter, for all his honors, became an increasingly isolated figure."[5]

This was not the theme of the 1983 first edition, to which the second edition bears only passing resemblance. Although the two volumes are approximately equal in size, the second edition attempts to contextualize Carter's entire career—for the most part in terms of its "American" versus its "European" aspects—in an introduction of just thirty-three pages before launching into more or less detailed discussions of individual works arranged chronologically according to performing forces. In contrast, the first edition spends well over half its length on an overview of Carter's intellectual and philosophical concerns before moving on to an account of Carter's career that deals with each composition in turn.

At least some of the chapter titles of the first edition promise insights into the real essence and the driving forces of Carter's music. The second and third chapters, for example, are titled "Musical Time: Rhythm and Form" and "Musical Space: Texture and Harmony"; even more tantalizing, the narrative's last five chapters, occasionally borrowing from literary sources or titles of Carter compositions, are labeled "Voyages," "Supreme Fictions," "Ideas of Disorder," "The Music of Our Climate," and "Music and Poetry." For some readers, Schiff delivered exactly what he promised; for others, especially academic readers steeped in music theory, Schiff's book was a severe disappointment.

The book resembles "a nightmarishly long program note [that] substitutes adoring panegyrics for objective criticism," wrote composer Charles Wuorinen in his review for the *Musical Quarterly*.[6] Robert P. Morgan in the *Journal of Musicology* similarly complained that Schiff seems to have approached his subject from "an essentially uncritical perspective."[7] British musicologist Arnold Whittall, in *Music & Letters*, praised the colorful language with which Schiff often described Carter's music yet challenged the "rather superficial, selective approach to the individual compositions."[8] In the *Musical Times* another British writer, David Harvey, noted that "the writing is rarely analytical in any critical sense" and that Schiff's enthusiasm for certain works "sometimes leads him to make exaggerated claims."[9] In the *Journal of the American Musicological Society*, composer/theorist Robert Morris decried Schiff's "statements that smack of idolatry" before, more pointedly, observing that by not comparing Carter with other composers Schiff "implies that it is primarily Carter alone who has brought new music to where it is today."[10]

But no matter how much they quibbled with Schiff's arguably uncritical approach and the relative shallowness of his musical analyses, all the reviewers just cited somewhere along the line acknowledged Carter's position in the existing musical hierarchy. Lest they, too, be accused of being adulatory, the reviewers tended to be cautious with their superlatives. Carter, they wrote, is "certainly *among* America's most gifted and eminent composers," an artist who over the past few decades "has emerged as *one of* the world's most important composers."[11] And with these comments, directed not toward the book at hand but toward its subject, the reviewers in effect confirmed Schiff's unstated but nonetheless fairly clear purpose.

Whatever its analytical flaws or editorial biases, Schiff's 1983 *The Music of Elliott Carter* was the first book-length treatment of music by an incontestably "major" composer who by the time of the book's publication was already in his midseventies. That it prompted as much attention as it did—overwhelmingly favorable reviews in the popular press by critics who affiliated with contemporary music, hair-splitting discussions by representatives of the possibly agenda-laden academic press—simply amplified the stature that Carter had already been granted with his two Pulitzer Prizes and his recent Siemens award. And the theme of the book, as much obvious to its supporters as to its detractors, was celebratory.

The theme of the 1998 second edition is different. It is articulated explicitly only in the book's introduction, but it is implied rather constantly not just by what Schiff has to say about *In Sleep, in Thunder* and other newer works but also by what he chooses to delete from his commentaries on older works. Perhaps as a result of the author's earlier trouncing, gone from the second edition are almost all of the grand pronouncements about the striking originality of this or that Carterian concept. Instead of bold statements about incomparable brilliance one finds hint upon hint—usually in accounts of post-1980 compositions but sometimes in references to earlier music as well—that Carter's worldview in his later years was growing darker and darker.

Such an assessment would seem to mesh with certain ideas put forth by Edward Said, who in his posthumous *On Late Style: Music and Literature against the Grain* dealt both with the concept of "artistic lateness not as harmony and resolution but as intransigence, difficulty, and unresolved contradiction" and with "the experience of late style that involves a nonharmonious, nonserene tension, and above all, a sort of deliberately unproductive productiveness going *against*. . . ."[12] After all, Carter at the time of the premiere of *In Sleep, in Thunder* was seventy-three years old, by chronological measurement certainly old enough to have entered the last of what Said calls the "three great human episodes common to all cultures and traditions."[13]

But an assessment that has Carter, in his seventies and onward, playing the role of embittered exile does not agree much with the actual music that Carter produced in his "late" period. And such an assessment contradicts what Schiff himself sometimes says about this music. It may well be that Carter, in private conversations with Schiff, shared thoughts about his perceived "isolation." Nevertheless, and notwithstanding *In Sleep, in Thunder*'s very deliberate exploration of the "dark side" of human nature, through most of his late period, Schiff writes, "Carter has been drawn to the idea of lightness."[14]

This is not to suggest that Carter's later works are breezy toss-offs; even Carter's one and only excursion into opera—the 1998 *What Next?*—for all its apparent comedy has underpinnings that are musically as well as psychologically serious. But the later compositions, doubtless owing both to "a new fluency" in Carter's working methods and a new penchant for shorter durations, were for the most part realized much more quickly than the three- and four-year projects of earlier years.[15] Whereas between 1960 and 1980 Carter completed only fifteen works, between 1980 and 2000 he completed almost fifty, and since 2001 he has completed at least three dozen more. More significant, many of Carter's later compositions, explicitly or not, seem to be musical representations of an intellectual quality that Italian novelist Italo Calvino called "lightness of thoughtfulness."

The idea was explored by Calvino in the first of the five essays that make up his *Six Memos for the Next Millennium*, intended to be the Charles Eliot Norton Lectures at Harvard University during the 1985–86 season but never delivered due to Calvino's death just before his planned departure for the United States. The five texts that Calvino had completed address the concepts of lightness, quickness, exactitude, visibility, and multiplicity; the sixth text—intended to be written while the writer was in residence at Harvard—was to have dealt with consistency. Together, these half-dozen "virtues" would, Calvino hoped, sustain literature against the promised technological onslaughts of the twenty-first century. Calvino called them "peculiarities of literature," but most of them apply just as well to music.[16]

Exactitude, multiplicity, and consistency had played a part in Carter's music even in the late 1940s, and they became increasingly evident as the years went on. These three "virtues" are to a large extent what makes possible the "simultaneously interacting heterogeneous character-continuities" that Carter explicitly said formed the essence of his 1959 String Quartet No. 2 and that are abundantly observable in such later instrumental works as the Double Concerto (1961), the Piano Concerto (1965), the Concerto for Orchestra (1969), the String Quartet No. 3 (1971), the Duo for Violin and Piano (1974), the Brass Quintet (1974), and A Symphony of Three Orchestras (1976).[17] Multiplicities of musical material are perhaps not so apparent in the harmonically rich yet monosonic 1980 *Night Fantasies* for piano or in the text-dominated *A Mirror on Which to Dwell* (1975), *Syringa* (1978), and *In Sleep, in Thunder* (1981). Yet these compositions, too, are governed throughout by rigorously consistent rhythmic and pitch-related procedures, and certainly in every detail they are realized with painstaking exactitude.

Visibility is the only one of Calvino's six virtues that does not easily find a parallel in music, for Calvino seems to use the word quite literally, in reference to vivid word-spun images of the sort that figure so strikingly into such of his novels as *Invisible Cities* (1972) and *If on a Winter's Night a Traveler* (1979). But certainly there is a musical equivalent of quickness, which for Calvino has to do not with mere technical facility or glibness but with the almost instantaneous mental process that "communicates something special that is derived simply from its very swiftness."[18] And certainly there is a musical equivalent—especially pertinent in many of Carter's later works—of lightness.

Alluding to an episode from Boccaccio's *Decameron* in which a clever poet delivers a potent verbal barb and then escapes his foes by jumping over a tomb, Calvino notes that it offers "an auspicious image" for the new millennium: "the sudden agile leap of the poet-philosopher who raises himself above the weight of the world, showing that with all his gravity he has the secret of lightness, and that what many consider to be the vitality of the times—noisy, aggressive, revving, and roaring—belongs to the realm of death, like a cemetery for old cars."[19]

The lightness that Calvino so hopefully celebrates results not from "vagueness and the haphazard" but, rather, from "precision and determination." Nor is it the same as frivolity, which when compared with examples of genuine "thoughtful lightness" can often "seem dull and heavy." Calvino discusses three types of literary lightness, the first of which has to do with the texture of a writer's language and the third of which has to do with verbal imagery. It is really only Calvino's second type of lightness—manifest in the flow of "the narration of a train of thought or psychological process" and suggestive of a work's many "subtle and imperceptible elements"—that finds an analogue in Carter's music.[20]

Apparently finding in *Six Memos for the Next Millennium* ideas that resonated sympathetically with his own current thinking, Carter borrowed from Calvino's book a key phrase and used it in 1990 as the title of a short piece for clarinet, violin, and cello whose subtitle explicitly declares it to be an homage to Calvino. Perhaps in part because the work was commissioned by an Italian organization, Carter opted to keep the Calvino phrase in its original language. And he cannily prefaced Calvino's two-word construction with a preposition of the sort that suggests the title is a performance directive, an instruction to the players regarding the general approach they should take to the written notes; just as so many composers in the past had asked musicians to effect certain passages "with love" (*con amore*) or "with ferocity" (*con fuoco*), in this case Carter seems to be advising his trio to realize the entire piece "with lightness of thought." At the same time, the title—*Con leggerezza pensosa*—can be read not just as a summary of the musical content of this particular piece but as a general description of the new direction that Carter's music had lately taken.

There is of course nothing "light" about *In Sleep, in Thunder.* But Carter's next composition, the 1982 Triple Duo, projects an attitude that surely must have taken Carter devotees by surprise. The piece begins with a practical joke that is almost the reverse of the one Haydn pulled with his "Farewell" Symphony; whereas Haydn's piece ends with the players one by one quitting the stage, Carter's begins with the players going through the motions of warming up, and after that the music's "high spirits and slapstick pacing never let up."[21]

Numerous other examples demonstrate that the concept of "play," as Arnold Whittall has put it, had become "a privileged image" for Carter, something "fundamental to the remarkably positive, optimistic tone that seems to pervade his later compositions."[22] Carter's 1985 *Penthode,* for five diverse quintets, mimics the tripartite structure of an eighteenth-century da capo aria and features an "extraordinary cadential gesture [that is] a parody of an operatic cadenza."[23] The 1987 Oboe Concerto features a soloist who right from the start embodies the very "idea of lightness" and eventually "seems to teach the orchestra how to 'lighten up.'"[24] In the 1990 Violin Concerto, Carter "takes the ideal of thoughtful lightness even further, achieving . . . a Mendelssohnian lucidity" based on stark contrasts between a dense orchestral backdrop and the soloist's increasingly effervescent material.[25] Carter's own program note for the London premiere of the 1991 Quintet for Piano and Winds mentions the work's "interplay of commentary, answer, [and] humorous denial" that is often "ironic, supporting, or self-effacing."[26] In the 1993 *Gra,* for solo clarinet, "playfulness is . . . explicit, from the initial marking, 'ghiribizzoso' (whimsical, capricious), and [the] material that seems to portray laughing dismissals of brief expressive sighs."[27] The title of the clarinet piece translates, from the Polish, as "play"; in the same vein, the title of the 1993 *Partita* for orchestra (the first of three movements that in 1998 would be presented together as *Symphonia*) alludes not to sixteenth-century sets of variations or eighteenth-century suites but to the modern Italian term for a soccer scrimmage. Carter's 1994 *90+* for solo piano features "explosions and excursions which traverse the keyboard's extremes with gleeful insouciance."[28] The overall "tone" of his 1996 Clarinet Concerto seems clearly enough established by the initial directives *scherzando* and *giocoso.*

Displays of good humor, many of them quite overt, indeed figure into Carter's later work. Yet despite their apparent levity, or perhaps because of it, the later compositions also demonstrate Carter's trademark gravitas. Music that is somehow perceived as "light" in weight, color, or expressive content seems all the more so when contrasted with music somehow perceived as "dark." Interested since the mid-1940s in articulating different strands of musical thought presented simultaneously, Carter in the 1980s and 1990s extended his repertoire to include not just contrasts based on pitch, rhythm, and gesture but also—to a much greater extent than ever before—contrasts based on overall musical affect. Perhaps taking a cue from Titian, Tintoretto, and other Renaissance painters whose canvases are notable for bold juxtaposition of illumination and shadow, Carter in his late period indulged liberally in the musical equivalent of chiaroscuro.

For Schiff, dramatic conflicts between "light" solo material and "dark" accompaniments represent "the Carterian pathos of isolation" that informs virtually all of the composer's later works.[29] But the sonic lightness of Carter's later music and the "lightness of thought" that seems to have generated it can be interpreted in a way that seems less ominous. Carter's 1994 *Of Challenge and of Love*, a setting for soprano and piano of poetry by John Hollander, ends its penultimate section with a remarkably transparent treatment of these lines from Hollander's "Quatrains from Harp Lake":

> Words of pure winter, yet not pinched nor mean;
> Blue truth can handle a good deal of gray.
> Dulled, but incontrovertibly still green,
> The noble laurel holds the cold at bay.

"The image," writes Whittall, "seems to be that of aging stoically, with the determination to resist decay and the satisfaction of knowing that the 'truth' of one's beliefs and capabilities need not be seriously eroded by the passing of time."[30] And perhaps this image applies to Carter's view of himself during his later years.

The examples of "late style" that interested Edward Said—manifest in the music of Beethoven and Schoenberg or in the literary efforts of Henrik Ibsen and Jean Genet—are expressive of anger and disillusion. Examples of late style in which Said admittedly was not interested come from the likes of Shakespeare and Verdi, who seem to have entered their twilight with "a spirit of reconciliation and serenity" and who produced "works that exude not so much a spirit of wise resignation as a renewed, almost youthful energy that attests to an apotheosis of artistic creativity and power."[31] In light of all its *leggerezza pensosa*, Carter's later music clearly falls into this latter category.

Carter's New Classicism?

In a 1994 on-line note for Boosey & Hawkes, the London-based music publisher with whom Carter affiliated beginning with *In Sleep, in Thunder*, Jonathan W. Bernard points out that "Carter has arrived at a working method that is in some sense definitive, a summa of all that has preceded it—or, as some have called it, a 'new classicism.'"[32]

To call Carter's late-period working method a "summa" of all that came before is a positive way of referring to what less than charitable critics might have termed a cessation of growth. Growth had certainly been a feature of Carter's earlier career, beginning with the seminal works of the 1940s and continuing for the next thirty-five years. As Bernard had noted elsewhere, Carter's musical growth involved "no rapid or radical shift in technique" but, rather, a gradual process in which "nearly every successive composition" expanded upon harmonic-rhythmic procedures explored in the previous composition.[33] Many sympathetic observers of contemporary music after the twentieth century's midpoint not only expected but took comfort in this slow but sure forward movement. In his review of the first edition of Schiff's book, Robert P. Morgan observed that, in large part because of a "stylistic evolution [that] has shown a remarkable consistency and logical progression," "there is something reassuring about the music of Elliott Carter."[34]

Once Carter had made the fundamental decision to write music based on the simultaneous presentation of different flows of activity, for a long while he consistently and logically developed the various rhythmic and pitch-related techniques that made such stratification possible. That being the case, an account of Carter's music from 1955 through 1980 might easily be cast in the form of a litany of technical innovations. Carter being obviously capable of devising ever new ways of using pitch sets and rhythms to inform "auditory scenarios . . . for performers to act out with their instruments," one has to wonder why, after the 1980 *Night Fantasies,* he did not simply continue along this proven path.[35]

One reason might be that Carter felt that his hitherto relentless drive toward technical innovation had finally reached a point of diminishing returns. Reflecting back on a work he had vigorously championed in the early 1970s not just as a critic but as a performer, Samuel Lipman in 1987 wrote that

> the Piano Concerto of Elliott Carter, in its level of complexity and dissonance, in its rapidity of movement and change, in the demands it makes on both performers and audience, securely occupies the line separating viable from non-viable music. In my own life, I am afraid I have chosen to stay on the near side of this line, even when that has meant giving up the hope of greatness I once entertained for Carter's music. Others, doubtless, perhaps more adventurous by nature, will put the line of arability on the other side of Carter. I have no doubt at all that whatever the fate of Carter's mature works may be, composition cannot go further in the direction he has adumbrated and remain what can be recognized as music.[36]

It seems unlikely that Carter saw himself, to use Richard Taruskin's colorful phrase, going down "a cul-de-sac [filled with] absurdly overcomposed monstrosities."[37] It is possible, however, that Carter, after having moved further and further in the direction of complexity, eventually shared Lipman's opinion that the results of constant technical innovation were no longer musically "arable." And it is also possible—quite likely, all things considered—that Carter in the early 1980s simply no longer felt the need "to develop virtually a new language for every piece."[38]

Carter as much as confirmed this in an interview conducted shortly before his hundredth birthday. In the 1960s and 1970s, Carter said, he "used to write these gigantic pieces that were very complex and took a long time to compose, if not to play. . . . Those pieces were me working out certain ideas about music. Those ideas are now part of my life, so I don't have to think about them in quite the same way."[39] In a 1996 interview, Carter stated that the extramusical substance of his work had in fact not changed much since the end of World War II. Generalizing about *all* the music he had produced since then, he said that "the notion of the experience of time" was always at the heart of it:

> I have tried in my pieces to give the concept of the passage of time as a dramatic idea, so that the pieces change as they go along in one way or another; different kinds of rhythm conflict with each other and so on. This was a sense that I wanted to give because after all, as we live our own lives, we are constantly involved in all sorts of different aspects of time. What's happening now, what's going on in our head about what's happening now, which is also something about the past and something about the future, and how we feel about all of this. So that is what I've done.[40]

This is indeed what Carter had done, and what even as a centenarian he continues to do. But a crucial difference between Carter's earlier work and his work from 1980 onward is the purpose that this music served for Carter. One hesitates to use the term *étude* to describe such finely wrought masterworks as the String Quartet No. 2 or A Symphony of Three Orchestras. Yet in a sense these were for Carter, like the counterpoint exercises he had penned under the strict tutelage of Nadia Boulanger, study pieces through which ever more difficult compositional problems were posed and then solved. And it seems that Carter, after he finished *Night Fantasies*, felt that his lessons had finally been learned.

The "new classicism" to which Bernard referred has to do with more than a consolidation of musical techniques that Carter had laboriously developed over the previous half century. It also has to do with more than the facts that most of Carter's compositions since the early 1980s are relatively shorter than their predecessors, that they are by and large easier for performers to manage, and that many of them seem to be somehow informed by a "lightness of thought." For Bernard and others, Carter's new classicism is a perceivable musical quality, "among the hallmarks of which are a certain structural and formal directness, conveyed in textures that are almost transparent in their clarity."[41]

In connection with Carter, the term *new classicism* and its older variant, *neoclassicism*, began appearing with increasing frequency in journalistic reviews over the course of the 1980s. Carter indeed identified his early music as being neoclassical, but through most of his career he disavowed neoclassicism's underlying philosophy. In one of the questions posed for the 1971 *Flawed Words and Stubborn Sounds*, Allen Edwards reminded the composer that in a recent lecture he had compared musical neoclassicism to "music for a masquerade in a bomb-shelter," and later Carter "recogniz[ed] the neoclassic impulse as one born of a misguided and ultimately futile attempt to take refuge in the past."[42]

Attempting both to summarize what critics had lately been hearing and to clarify the language that might be used to describe it, Schiff in 1989 published an article titled "Carter's New Classicism." Lest anyone get the mistaken impression that Carter's current music somehow exemplified a throwback to archaic structural patterns or even to the tonal music that Carter himself wrote in the late 1930s and early 1940s, Schiff starts out by making the strong point that, to his ears, Carter's recent work "sounds as resolutely modernist as ever."[43] Then he launches into an exploration of the role that classic art has played, or might play, in the culture of the late twentieth century. Instead of contrasting the concept of classic art (controlled, formalist, Apollonian in its ideals) with its familiar opposite, that is, romantic art (freely expressive, adventurous in design, Dionysian in spirit), he weighs it against the concept of art that is somehow modern.

To preface his statement about Carter's recent music, Schiff draws generously from the classic-modern dichotomy as presented in the early 1970s by the French literary critic Roland Barthes.[44] Paraphrasing and sometimes directly quoting Barthes, Schiff writes:

> The classic text . . . is characterized by authority, mono-directionality, resolution; it is "closed" and its closure ensures the creation of what Barthes terms the "readerly text" in which the reader comfortably assumes that a work of fiction is presenting the world as it actually is. The classic text makes a hidden, coded claim of naturalness, of total, authoritative representation. The modern text by contrast is ambivalent, multi-directional, and "open" or—as Barthes says—"plural." . . . The modern text demands the creation by the active reader of what Barthes calls the "writerly text." Because of its gaps and aporia it requires that the reader be "no longer a consumer but a producer of the text."[45]

The idea of the modern "open" text and the active participation by readers that it invites was hardly unique to Barthes. Although focused not on literature but on media in general, a similar argument had dominated the writings of Canadian philosopher Marshall McLuhan in the 1960s, and in the same decade discussions of "openness" in various art forms had been undertaken by the Italian philosopher Umberto Eco. Later, the concept of openness would become one of the central tenets of the trend known as the postmodern.

In a 1996 article that sought to enumerate the ways in which so-called postmodern music might manifest itself, Jonathan Kramer included as the last two items on his list the observations that postmodern music sometimes "presents multiple meanings and multiple temporalities" and "locates meaning and even structure in listeners, more than in scores, performances, or composers."[46] But even in the 1980s it was starting to be acknowledged that "postmodernism is a maddeningly imprecise musical concept," that the term *postmodern* is "something of a catchall and susceptible to mere modishness," and that "defining" postmodern music "is a notorious fool's errand."[47] The term being so slippery, it is surprising that Schiff introduced a hyphenated variant of it into his discussion of Carter's "new classicism."

Referring to four of Carter's larger recent works (the 1983 Triple Duo, the 1985 *Penthode*, the 1986 String Quartet No. 4, the 1987 Oboe Concerto), Schiff writes that each of these "explores the relationship between the givens of the modern text and an imagined transcendence of the conditions of modernism in the direction of what might be termed a post-modern classicism—if, and only if, we mean a classicism which has absorbed modernism, not an anti-modern restoration."[48] With this use of a verbal red herring, however much he tried to define it, Schiff muddied his argument.

The term seems to have been a distracting focal point for British critic Antony Bye, who early in a 1994 article titled "Carter's 'Classic' Modernism" barrages his readers with questions that are perhaps not entirely rhetorical. Assuming that few would disagree, Bye writes that Carter's works from the 1960s and 1970s "are explicitly, indeed vehemently, modernist." Then, provocatively, he asks: "But what of Carter's recent music, from the String Quartet No. 4 onwards? Is it true, as some commentators have suggested, that Carter's grip on modernism has weakened through an attempt to seek a rapprochement with those classical procedures he had long ago rejected? Is Carter's reaffirmation of his modernist credo simply the mechanical rehearsal of a position articulated by him many times before but of little relevance to his current compositional practice? Has Carter, in effect, become if not 'neo-classical' then at least 'post-modernist'?"[49]

Responding to his own questions before launching into a hopefully point-proving analysis of the 1993 *Gra*, Bye agrees with Schiff that Carter's recent music is neither neoclassical nor postmodern but, rather, representative of "a post-modern dialogue with 'classicism.'" He maintains that Carter's music is still, in both content and spirit, archly modernist. It may well be that the "outcome" of such works as the String Quartet No. 4 and the 1990 Violin Concerto is "less confrontational than in Carter's earlier music," but in these and later compositions "there is scarcely any sense of 'classical' resolution." As before, Bye writes, Carter in his recent work seeks to create music that for all its apparent chaos seeks "to exhibit a fundamental unity." It may be that certain of Carter's newer compositions seem to exhibit an "increase in Apollonian elements," but this "still does not imply an overriding 'classicism.'"[50]

Arnold Whittall, perhaps Britain's leading spokesman on all things having to do with Carter, has on numerous occasions addressed Schiff's view of Carter's new classicism. And almost always he has, like Bye, rejected it in favor of a view that sees the recent music simply as an extension, or variant, of Carter's long-championed modernism. In a 1992 review of the published score of Carter's Oboe Concerto, Whittall granted that, "as David Schiff in particular has argued," certain of Carter's later works (including the Oboe Concerto) seem to "have developed a more 'classical' concern with achieving a 'spirit of co-operation' between the participating groups and their materials." But this shift in compositional dynamics—representing not so much the logical development of materials as the presentation of materials in a "steady" state—nevertheless for Whittall suggests only "a change of emphasis" on Carter's part and not "a fundamental rejection of modernism in favor of a new classicism."[51]

Reflecting on the two movements of the projected *Symphonia: Sum Fluxae Pretium Spei* that had thus far been performed, Whittall several years later observed that the 1993 *Partita*—which, like the 1987 Oboe Concerto, seems as much "interested in working with homogeneity as with disparity"—at least to an extent approaches "that 'classical' ideal proposed by David Schiff as particularly relevant to the later Carter." Nevertheless, Whittall maintained, what "really drives" the "intricately exuberant musical discourse" of *Partita* and comparable works is not at all a "decisive shift" in aesthetic but a typically Carteresque "dialogue between modernist and classic [musical] qualities."[52]

Whittall notes that not just *Partita* but certain other of Carter's larger recent works—in particular the 1991 Quintet for Piano and Winds, the 1995 String Quartet No. 5, and the 1996 Clarinet Concerto—seem to avoid definitive statements and instead have about them a refreshing air of exploration, of "trying out" mere musical fragments. "In his music's marvelous Indian summer," Whittall writes, "such open-ended conclusiveness is Carter's way . . . of sustaining [his] modernist project, and of affirming its continuing viability." No matter how "fluent" Carter's methods might have become, and no matter how "lucid" his recent treatment of foreground materials, it remains that in Carter's work "the relish for a music that positively affirms its contemporaneity is still an abiding and sustaining force."[53]

Echoing Whittall and Bye, the American composer Ronald Caltabiano in 1998 argued that, contrary to prevailing theories of a new classicism, Carter's music in the previous decade had *not* fundamentally shifted course. "There is a line of thought, at least in his own country," Caltabiano wrote, that "Carter's music has gone through a tidal change in the last ten years, that he had finally given up on his crusade to demand Olympian feats of mental and aural skill to enjoy his music, that he had begun to give way—if only a little—to the trend toward simplicity that started with the neo-tonality of the late 1970s and the neo-Romanticism of the 1980s. In essence, that his music had finally become expressive in the traditional sense." Continuing the aqueous metaphor, Caltabiano insisted that "there has been no such sea change." To be sure, Carter's music had undergone audible changes over the previous decade. But these, Caltabiano claimed, simply represented "the careful, focused growth of the imagination and intellect of a musical giant."[54]

Applied to the various new directions in which Carter had moved since 1980, this argument perhaps holds water. After 1998, however, it seems that Carter's music *did* take a radical turn.

The "Season of Memory"

Penned on the eve of Carter's ninetieth birthday, Caltabiano's article briefly mentions the instrumental sextet *Luimen*, which had been presented in Amsterdam a few months earlier, and it notes that Carter's Quintet for Piano and Strings was awaiting its premiere and that Carter at the moment was correcting proofs for his one-act opera *What Next?* The most recent of Carter's works that Caltabiano discusses at length is *Symphonia: Sum Fluxae Pretium Spei*, the orchestral triptych that had had its first complete performance in April of that year. *Symphonia*, or at least the two-thirds of it that had already been heard, is also the latest work with which Whittall deals in his 1997 article, which reflects on the "long shadows" of Carter's "Indian summer." And *Symphonia* is the prime focus of a 1998 article in which Schiff examines all of Carter's orchestral music to date.

One suspects that it was not just because of its timing—or the anticipation generated by the fact that its components were offered to the public in piecemeal fashion and, in the case of the third movement, not without some controversy—

that *Symphonia* so powerfully attracted the attention of these different-minded writers.[55] Measured by chronometric time alone, the sixty-minute *Symphonia* fairly dwarfs not only Carter's earlier orchestral triptych (the 1989 *Three Occasions*) but also the orchestral works from Carter's "mature" period.[56] Measured by a more subjective criterion (e.g., philosophical scope or range of emotional content), *Symphonia* seems to "outweigh" even such substantial works as the Concerto for Orchestra and A Symphony of Three Orchestras. Whereas these and other of Carter's earlier masterpieces present, in effect, a diversity of characters embroiled in a single musical "drama," the *Symphonia* presents a multiplicity of dramas whose totality—but only when perceived *as* a totality—makes an especially strong impact. Carter's *Three Occasions* emerged as a triptych almost by happenstance, after conductor Oliver Knussen suggested to the composer that two earlier short works for orchestra might, if balanced by a third work of suitable character, make for a viable "package." In marked contrast, *Symphonia* right from the start was conceived as a large-scale work whose three movements would form "a deliberately unfinished symphony, a symphony without finale."[57]

Before rushing into an almost nonstop flurry of fast-moving exchanges between various instrumental groups, *Symphonia* begins, in its opening *Partita*, with a loudly blasted chord that contains the orchestra's highest and lowest possible pitches. After the middle movement, *Adagio tenebroso*, aptly described as "music of lyricism and reflection," "a work of endless sorrow," and "one of the few works in Carter's catalogue that is truly dark in character," the piece scuds through the lyrical *Allegro scorrevole* movement until it in effect evaporates in a barely audible high-register note played by a lone piccolo.[58] This is the very opposite of an emphatic cadence, yet it hardly seems—especially in the context of the two preceding movements—inconclusive. It may be that traditional Western music, following the eighteenth- and nineteenth-century models of most European languages, has long been in the habit of neatly wrapping up its discourse with the musical equivalent of a period. But twentieth-century modernist music, including Carter's, has often emulated a model especially favored by its contemporaneous Italian and French writers, that is, the ending of an important passage with deliberately provocative suspension points.

Apropos of *Symphonia*'s opening and closing gestures, it is tempting to think of the famously grim lines from part 5 of T. S. Eliot's 1925 *The Hollow Men:* "This is the way the world ends / Not with a bang but with a whimper." But the extra-musical message of Carter's *Symphonia* seems to be not nearly so apocalyptic. In size and scale *Symphonia* indeed has about it a quality of the "monumental." But what, one wonders, does it celebrate?

The fact that Carter came up with *Symphonia*'s subtitle (and the various lines that serve as epigraphs for each of the three movements) only *after* the complete triptych was being readied for performance raises the possibility, as Schiff has noted, of a deliberate attempt "to distract the listener from the work's ambitions." At any rate, the verbal material all comes from a Latin poem by the early seventeenth-century English metaphysical writer Richard Crashaw. *Symphonia*'s subtitle—"Sum fluxae pretium spei"—translates as "I am the prize of flowing hope," and such a line in any language seems cryptic. But simply from the poem's title—"Bulla," which translates as "bubble"—one gets the impression that Carter with the totality of *Symphonia* was perhaps paying homage, as Schiff suggests, not just to music's essence but to the essence of "all things fleeting and insubstantial."[59]

Recapitulating the dark theme that runs subtly throughout the second edition of *The Music of Elliott Carter*, Schiff in his 1998 article on Carter's symphonic music opines that the second movement of *Symphonia* is "a eulogy for all the devastation of the [twentieth] century."[60] Literary scholar Stephen Guy-Bray agrees with Schiff that Carter's *Symphonia*, like Crashaw's "Bulla," deals with the nature of the ephemeral, and he observes that the eight lines that Carter borrows from Crashaw all come from the lengthy poem's second half, "which is to say that they are more concerned with the rather depressing implications of transience than with the beauty of something that is transient." But "Schiff is on shakier ground," Guy-Bray writes, "when he states that 'the first two movements [of *Symphonia*] present the bright and dark sides of the 20th century in starkest contrast.'"[61] All things considered—including not just the music itself but also Carter's reference to humankind's efforts "to find a way of living in the midst of [the] appalling problems" of "this very turbulent century" in his acceptance speech for the 1981 Siemens Prize, his comment to a 1993 interviewer that "we are living in a world . . . completely changed by the writings of Freud," and his comments in 2004 to Dutch filmmaker Frank Scheffer to the effect that his and others' essays in musical modernism represented simply "a desire to find a more emphatic and stronger way of presenting . . . life as it was lived in the present time"—Schiff's statements do seem rather melodramatic.[62]

The 1998 *Symphonia* seems a skittishly framed eulogy for the twentieth century only if one takes the view, promoted by Schiff, that almost all of Carter's post-1980 music in ways more or less subtle expresses the feelings of an embittered and increasingly isolated American composer. Most listeners will doubtless experience *Symphonia* simply for what it is, that is, a masterly crafted large-scale orchestral work in which a somber midsection is flanked by a pair of dazzling scherzo movements. In interpreting *Symphonia* listeners will likely take the view, also promoted by Schiff, that it is a work not just of "mature compassion" but also of "youthful energy."[63]

Heard on its own, Carter's three-movement magnum opus for orchestra, which ends with a softly breathed "up in the air" piccolo note, hardly projects a tone of finality. The piece seems a valediction only when it is contemplated in light of what came next.

Carter's 1998 *What Next?* was inspired, the composer has often said in interviews, by a scene in Jacques Tati's 1971 comic film *Trafic* that shows a number of persons, their vehicles all suddenly damaged, ambling around in a daze. Aside from that seminal image, the one-act opera has nothing in common with the Tati film; whereas in *Trafic* the essentially harmless pile-up is just another inconvenience among the many misadventures experienced by a hapless gang trying to drive from Paris to Amsterdam, in *What Next?* a clearly serious accident—which, according to the libretto by British music journalist Paul Griffiths, need not at all be traffic related—is the immediate trigger of the characters' severe psychological disorientation. The opera's plot, if it can even be said to be a plot, centers on six persons' sometimes absurd but more often pathetic struggle to define not just themselves but their possible relationships to one another. As in Alain Resnais' film *Last Year at Marienbad*, the protagonists of Carter's *What Next?* exist in a perplexed state of knowing only that they *might* in some way be connected.

Like the diverse instrumental "characters" of Carter's dramatically conceived chamber music and works for orchestra, the opera's human characters are made distinct by unique collections of intervals and rhythmic gestures, and each of them over the course of forty minutes gets to hold forth spectacularly not just on his or her own but as a member of sharply stratified ensembles. According to Felix Meyer and Anne C. Shreffler, the majority of reviewers felt that Carter managed this stratification with a commendable "economy of means," but at least one "expressed the astonishing view" that most of the opera, in contrast to all the "lightness of thought" and "new classicism" arguably evident in Carter's music since the early 1980s, "harked back to [Carter's] ultracomplex style of the 1960s and '70s."[64]

In any case, *What Next?* involves a great deal of soul-baring revelation by characters who seem to be "taking themselves very seriously" and perhaps "suffer from terminal narcissism."[65] But except for an interlude during which a repair crew arrives to clear the wreckage and the protagonists collectively try to draw the workers' attention to themselves, the opera involves almost no action. Certainly it involves no dramatic or psychological development. At the opera's end the six characters are in the same sorry state they were in at the opera's start: they are still seeking to discover their identities, something they can only accomplish through the difficult act of willful remembering. And remembering, it seems, was much on Carter's mind during his tenth decade.

Although Carter had composed memorial pieces before—most notably the 1971 *Canon for 3*, the 1988 *Remembrance* for orchestra, and the 1994 *Fragment for String Quartet*, written "in memory," respectively, of Igor Stravinsky (1882–1971), music patron Paul Fromm (1906–87), and Boosey & Hawkes executive David Huntley (1947–94)—his "occasional" pieces typically honored persons who were very much alive. A few were written to celebrate special occasions: William Glock's 1984 retirement as director of the Bath Festival (recognized by Carter with his *Canon for 4: Homage to William*), for example, or the 1989 fiftieth anniversary of Carter and his wife's wedding (marked with the aptly titled *Anniversary* for orchestra). But the majority of them were birthday presents: the *Birthday Fanfare* (1978) for William Glock's seventieth and the *Birthday Flourish* (1988) for Carter's wife's eightieth, the two installments of *Esprit rude/esprit doux* (1984 and 1994) for Boulez's sixtieth and seventieth, *Riconoscenza per Goffredo Petrassi* (1984) and *90+* (1994) for Petrassi's eightieth and ninetieth, *Gra* (1993) for Witold Lutosławski's eightieth, *A Six Letter Letter* (1996) for Paul Sacher's ninetieth.

As happens with many healthy nonagenarians, Carter discovered after 1998 that he was outliving most of his friends. Of all the honorees just named, only Boulez, at the time of this writing, is still alive. Born in the same year as Carter, Glock passed away in 2000; four years younger than Carter, Petrassi died in 2003, and so did Carter's wife. Sacher was born in 1906 and died in 1999; Lutosławski was born in 1913 and died in 1994.

Rather than embarking on what might have been a depressingly long series of eulogies, Carter in his nineties produced just a handful of memorial pieces, each of them focusing on individuals who had been, early in his career, especially influential. In 1999 he wrote the solo violin pieces *Statement—Remembering Aaron* and *Fantasy—Remembering Roger*; in 2001 he wrote, for solo cello, *Figment II: Remembering Mr. Ives*. The titles alone of these tributes to Aaron Copland (1900–1990), Roger Sessions (1896–1985), and Charles Ives (1874–1954) neatly encapsulate Carter's view of his musical ancestry. It is a wonder that Carter has yet to write a tribute to Nadia Boulanger (1887–1979), but perhaps such a piece, as Carter moves into his eleventh decade, is in the works; on the other hand, perhaps Carter's homage is to be found in his decision in 2007 to revise yet again the almost seventy-year-old *Elegy*, which is so obviously a fruit of his work with Boulanger.[66]

Carter's preoccupation with remembering, after his ninetieth birthday, is evident to an extent in his occasional pieces that commemorate dead friends. But the preoccupation is much more evident in the literary inspirations for certain orchestral works and, more impressively, in his choice of texts for compositions that involve the human voice.

In the half century that separates his seminal Cello Sonata from his valedictory *Symphonia*, Carter wrote relatively little vocal music. *A Mirror on Which to Dwell*, *Syringa*, *In Sleep, in Thunder*, *Of Challenge and of Death*, and *What Next?*—the first three works clustered around the time of his seventieth birthday, the last two written in anticipation of his ninetieth—are in fact rare exceptions to Carter's characteristically instrumental mode of operation. But since 1998 Carter has composed no fewer than seven songs or song cycles, the first of which was initiated even while Carter was still at work on the opera.

Especially in contrast to the vocal writing in the opera, which in its angularity and rich counterpoint resembles the style of Carter's mature works for chamber ensembles, the lyrical writing not just for voice but for the accompanying instruments in *Tempo e tempi* represents a remarkable shift in style. As Meyer and Shreffler rightly observe, "the brevity, simplicity, and emotional directness of this song cycle are worlds away from the multilayered complexity typical of much of Carter's previous music"; indeed, they write, *Tempo e tempi* "anticipates several features of Carter's more recent music and may even mark the point at which one could say that his 'late style' begins."[67]

The idea for *Tempo e tempi* came from Raffaele Pozzi, the director of the Pontino Festival whose urgings had earlier brought about *Con leggerezza pensosa* and the *Immer neu* for oboe and harp. In the spring of 1998 Pozzi sent Carter a pair of poems by Eugenio Montale, the Italian poet who in 1975 had won the Nobel Prize for Literature. The poem that lent its title to what eventually became a group of eight songs begins with a statement that must have seemed particularly relevant to an eighty-nine-year-old composer who had spent most of his adult life devising ways in which the experience of "psychological time" might somehow be represented through music: "Non c'è un unico tempo: ci sono molti nastri che paralleli slittano spesso in senso contrario e raramente s'intersecano" (There is not just one time: its many tapes run parallel to one another but frequently in opposite directions, and they rarely intersect).[68]

Carter's setting of the poem—for soprano, violin, English horn, and bass clarinet—was premiered at the Pontino Festival on 1 July 1998. Once *What Next?*

was finished, Carter turned to the second Montale poem ("L'Arno a Rovezzano") and then found six more Italian poems (two by Salvatore Quasimodo, four by Giuseppe Ungaretti) that, like "Tempo e tempi," in one way or another reflect on the passage of time. With woodwind parts that involve doublings on oboe and clarinet and with the accompanying ensemble expanded to include cello, the song cycle, which perhaps represents the start of Carter's "late style," was completed just a month before the 16 September 1999 premiere in Berlin of the opera, which perhaps represents the last vestiges of his "mature" style.

Along with the several memorial pieces mentioned above, Carter's instrumental music since his ninetieth birthday includes compositions for solo piano (the 1999 *Two Diversions;* the 2000 *Retrouvailles;* the 2005 *Intermittences* and the 2006 *Caténaires*, which were linked as *Two Thoughts about the Piano;* and—written for conductor/pianist James Levine in honor of various of his family members—the curiously titled 2007 *Matribute* and the 2008 *Fratribute* and *Sistribute*), concertos or concerto-like compositions (the 2000 *ASKO Concerto* and Cello Concerto; the 2003 *Dialogues* for piano and large ensemble; the 2006 Horn Concerto; the 2007 *Interventions* for piano and orchestra; and the 2008 Flute Concerto), pieces for conventional chamber ensemble (the 1999 *Fragment No. 2* for string quartet; the 2001 Oboe Quartet; and the 2007 Clarinet Quintet), pieces for solo instruments or unconventional small combinations (the 2001 *Hiyoku* for two clarinets and *Steep Steps* for solo bass clarinet; the 2002 *Retracing* for solo bassoon and *Au Quai* for bassoon and viola; the 2003 *Call* for horn and two trumpets; the 2007 *HBHH* for solo oboe, *Figment III* for solo contrabass, and *Figment IV* for solo viola; and the 2008 *Tintinnabulation* for percussion sextet and the *Duettino* for violin and cello), and works for orchestra or other large ensemble (the 2002 *Boston Concerto* and *Micomicón;* the 2004 *Réflexions*, *Mosaic*, *More's Utopia*, and *Fons juventatis;* the 2005 *Soundings;* the 2007 *Sound Fields* for strings; and the 2008 *Wind Rose* for twenty-four woodwind instruments).[69]

Impressive as this prolific outpouring of instrumental music is, it pales in light of Carter's very recent music for voice. Along with the 1999 *Tempo e tempi*, the songs or song cycles that so clearly articulate the essence of Carter's late style include the 2002 *Of Rewaking* (settings for mezzo-soprano and orchestra of poems by William Carlos Williams), the 2006 *In the Distances of Sleep* (settings for mezzo-soprano and large chamber ensemble of poems by Wallace Stevens), the 2007 *Mad Regales* (settings for six solo voices of poems by John Ashbery), the 2007 *La Musique* (a setting for unaccompanied soprano of a short poem by Charles Baudelaire), the 2008 *On Conversing with Paradise* (settings for baritone and chamber orchestra of poems by Ezra Pound), and the 2008 *Poems of Louis Zukofsky* (for soprano and clarinet).

Without diminishing their quality of craftsmanship or their fundamental musicality, one might say of Carter's many late-style instrumental works not just that they are all of a piece but also that, collectively as well as individually, they are not nearly so compelling as the relatively few instrumental works that Carter laboriously produced in the 1950s, 1960s, and 1970s. Summarizing Carter's late style, John Link has observed that "in recent years Carter has disavowed the analogy between his music and the theatrical stage, preferring to emphasize the collaborative nature of chamber music performance. His recent harmonic practice, in which the instruments share a common harmonic vocabulary, has unfixed the identity of the instrument and character and made it a variable subject of manipulation."[70] With this consolidation of harmony, Carter has indeed effected a nontonal style that—so long as its manifestations are relatively short—is easy enough on the ears. But Carter's newest instrumental compositions deliberately avoid the confrontations of his earlier work; the music is lyrical and shapely, but seldom does it demand concentrated listening.

The situation in Carter's recent song cycles is altogether different. In these works, as in the venerable song cycles by such nineteenth-century composers as Schubert and Schumann, the goal is to let the human voice not just clearly deliver the texts at hand but also somehow "express" the texts' most subtle nuances, with the instrumental accompaniments not arguing but only lending empathetic support. *Mad Regales* and *La Musique*, of course, have no instrumental accompaniment, but only *Mad Regales*—its title a playful Ashberian corruption of the word *madrigals* and its music imitative, albeit in distinctly Carteresque fashion, of the dense weaves of sixteenth-century polyphony—is really an exception. In all the other pieces, it seems that foremost in the composer's mind has been the patently simple and essentially declamatory presentation of a potent text.

The text of *La Musique* reflects on the bittersweet experience of listening to music that is, by its very nature, evanescent. The three poems by William Carlos Williams that provide Carter with the emotional-philosophical substance for *Of Rewaking* deal, as Link writes, "in various ways with a central conundrum of human life: nature renews itself each year, but we do not."[71] All six of the Wallace Stevens poems that Carter sets in *In the Distances of Sleep* likewise touch on ideas of evanescence and renewal, but the gist of Carter's thinking throughout his tenth decade is perhaps best represented in the poem—"Puella Parvula"—with which Carter begins the song cycle:

Every thread of summer is at last unwoven.
By one caterpillar is great Africa devoured
And Gibraltar is dissolved like spit in the wind.
But over the wind . . .
. . . the mighty imagination triumphs
Like a trumpet and says, in this season of memory,
When the leaves fall like things mournful of the past,
Keep quiet in the heart, O wild bitch.

Carter's treatment of this particular poem is definitely confrontational, and his setting of the above-quoted excerpt's last three words—with the ensemble falling silent and the mezzo-soprano allowed an ad libitum sneer—implies that his own relationship with both past and present is perhaps not without conflict. But later in the song cycle Carter's music progressively relaxes, suggesting not an attitude of resignation but simply one of thoughtful acceptance. The last song in the cycle bears the title "God Is Good. It Is a Beautiful Night"; appropriately, Carter's music, with the mezzo-soprano ascending gently to the heights, generates an air of almost beatific calm.

Epilogue

IN A REVIEW OF THE 1988 REISSUE in paperback of David Schiff's book, H. Wiley Hitchcock remarked, almost casually, that "it is difficult to generalize about Carter's music and what makes it tick."[1] Such a statement might apply to any composer, but it seems especially true when applied to a composer who has lived as long and has been as productive as Carter. Still, generalizations about Carter abound.

Schiff's most sweeping generalization comes in the 1998 second edition of *The Music of Elliott Carter*, and with it he stands virtually alone in suggesting that Carter's music, especially from the twentieth century's last two decades and perhaps some of the earlier music as well, is darkened by shades of bitterness and isolation. Likewise focusing on Carter's recent music but hearing in it large measures of brightness, Leon Botstein writes that "the dense complexity of [Carter's] music of the mid-century has given way to a clarity and translucence," and John Link generalizes that Carter has lately "developed a lighter comic touch" that is balanced by "a clear-eyed, though poignant, wistfulness."[2] A similar idea is found in an account by Arnold Whittall of Carter's 2008 opera, but it is expressed in such a way that it fairly nails the governing spirit of almost all of Carter's mature work.

Comparing Carter to Pierre Boulez, Whittall suggests that the music of both composers for decades has been profoundly affected by the "abiding influence" of their "Gallic mentors," in Boulez's case Olivier Messiaen and in Carter's case Nadia Boulanger. Messiaen and Boulanger were in many ways as different as are Boulez and Carter, yet the two of them "shared an aesthetic ethos that resisted the projection of alienated melancholia." For all its seriousness, Whittall writes, Carter's music since the middle of the twentieth century has maintained a tone that is "predominantly upbeat."[3]

Of course, not all Carter commentators have been so generous. As noted earlier, Richard Taruskin has described Carter's works (and also the serial works of Milton Babbitt) as "absurdly overcomposed monstrosities." Trying perhaps too hard to make his point, Taruskin sets up Carter as the target of an entire chapter of the fifth volume of his huge *Oxford History of Western Music*. Whereas Benjamin Britten for Taruskin personifies the socially aware, socially engaged twentieth-century artist whose music appeals to large audiences and in almost every way reflects on or responds to the world around him, Carter (like Babbitt) personifies the opposite, the aloof artisan whose deliberately "difficult" work has nothing at all to do with the real world and primarily serves "fellow composers, performers, scholars, and academically inclined or affiliated critics" as "a touchstone of self-congratulation."[4] To lend extra ammunition to his favored side in the Britten-Carter "standoff," Taruskin quotes out of context one of Carter's most stalwart champions, pianist Charles Rosen, in a way that makes it seem as though Rosen is claiming that the worthiness of Carter's music is proved by the fact that so many people find it incomprehensible.[5] And this is exactly the sort of thing one would expect from a performer, Taruskin says, who like Carter has long been both a willing participant in and beneficiary of the "prestige machine."[6]

However one views Taruskin's invocation of Rosen here and elsewhere, it is true that Rosen has often professed the belief that when complex music is also good music it behooves serious listeners to make an effort.[7] Only when the language of music so knotty as Carter's is thoroughly learned can it be adequately heard, Rosen wrote in his 2009 belated centennial tribute to his friend; only when "one understands how the music works" can one "perceive the [music's] emotion."[8]

Just as Taruskin's generalization has it that the music of Carter is cold and bloodless, so Rosen's standard generalization describes the music as impassioned and deeply meaningful. But Rosen has also generalized about Carter in a more objective way. Remarking not on the expressive content of Carter's music but only on its treatment of pitch and rhythm, Rosen told the Dutch filmmaker Frank Scheffer that Carter is

> the only composer who actually synthesizes the two great traditions of the earlier part of the twentieth century, . . . the first composer to see to what extent the whole Stravinsky

tradition, and what came out of Boulanger, could be combined with all of the great influences of the other school of music [i.e., the highly organized serial music of Schoenberg] that went on at that time. But there was a price that had to be paid. In a sense, the solution was to reject most of the doctrine of both schools. And something very original comes out, which sounds . . . very American and at the same time very specifically integrated into the European tradition. And that seems, to me, very extraordinary.[9]

A longer discussion might fruitfully explore the question of just how "American," and in what ways, Carter's music really is. It might explore, too, the nature and extent of the relationship between certain instrumental works and the quotations from poetry that Carter in one way or another has attached to them—not just the Crashaw "Bulla" that accompanies *Symphonia*, for example, but also the Petrarch line that gives *Scrivo in vento* its title, the Rilke fragment that serves as a motto for *Trilogy*, the Robert Lowell "Myopia: A Night," whose essence Carter compared to that of *Night Fantasies*, the "Vents" of St. John Perse that Carter says illuminates the Concerto for Orchestra, "The Bridge" of Hart Crane that clearly inspired A Symphony of Three Orchestras. And a longer discussion might delve deeply into both similarities and differences between "fluid" time as manifest in Carter's music and comparable representations in cinema and other art forms.

But this, by contractual necessity, is a short book. It began with an introduction that readers can take to be my own generalization as to what makes Carter's music "tick." Along with an account of Carter's life and a compact survey of his work, the book has featured a good many of Carter's own generalizations, and it can close with a few more, a pair that I think summarize the essence of Carter's music far more succinctly than could any technical exegesis.

Technical details, as it happened, were precisely what Benjamin Boretz was trying to elicit when he interviewed Carter in the fall of 1968 at New York University as part of a series of public "conversations" with leading modernist composers. Carter responded dutifully and at length to questions about his use of pitch sets, metric flow, counterpoint, instrumentation, and texture, but he began to resist when asked to give a clinical explanation of his music's unifying concepts. At last giving in, he said: "The idea of my music, if it can be considered apart from its expressive and communicative character (which I doubt), could be said to be a constantly evolving series of shapes, like the patterns of choreography." Pressed further, he added: "My musical attitude did not arise from a desire to compose a certain kind of music, 'original' or otherwise. Rather it came directly from my own human experience and thoughts about it, corroborated by St. Augustine,

A. N. Whitehead[,] . . . and others. I have been in search of a music that would embody the human experience of process and its transcendence."[10]

And those two images—the "constantly evolving series of shapes" and the "human experience of process"—are perhaps the best keys available for anyone seeking to make his or her own generalizations about Elliott Carter.

NOTES

Introduction

1. Carter, "Music and the Time Screen," in *The Writings of Elliott Carter*, ed. Else Stone and Kurt Stone (Bloomington: Indiana University Press, 1977), 363–64; and in Jonathan W. Bernard, ed., *Elliott Carter: Collected Essays and Lectures, 1937–1995* (Rochester, N.Y.: University of Rochester Press, 1997), 280.

2. Most of Carter's essays are gathered in the two collections cited in note 1; commentary of a more informal sort, cast in the form of a book-length interview, appears in Allen Edwards, *Flawed Words and Stubborn Sounds: A Conversation with Elliott Carter* (New York: W. W. Norton, 1971).

3. Elliott Carter, liner note for *Sonata for Cello and Piano*, Nonesuch 79183 (1968), in Stone and Stone, *Writings*, 269; Bernard, *Elliott Carter*, 228.

4. David Schiff, *The Music of Elliott Carter*, 1st ed. (London: Eulenburg, 1983), 138–42.

CHAPTER 1. *Foundations (1908–45)*

1. Richard Franko Goldman, "The Music of Elliott Carter," *Musical Quarterly* 43, no. 2 (1957): 152.

2. Carter, in Allen Edwards, *Flawed Words and Stubborn Sounds: A Conversation with Elliott Carter* (New York: W. W. Norton, 1971), 42–43.

3. Ibid., 43–44.

4. Carter, "Charles Ives Remembered" (1974), in *The Writings of Elliott Carter*, ed. Else Stone and Kurt Stone (Bloomington: Indiana University Press, 1977), 259; and in *Elliott Carter: Collected Essays and Lectures, 1937–1995*, ed. Jonathan W. Bernard (Rochester, N.Y.: University of Rochester Press, 1997), 99.

5. Ibid.

6. Carter, "Documents of a Friendship with Ives," *Parnassus* 3, no. 2 (1975): 300, in Stone and Stone, *Writings*, 331; in Bernard, *Elliott Carter*, 107.

7. Ibid.

8. Charles Ives to the dean of admissions at Harvard University, 1926, in Stone and Stone, *Writings*, 331; in Bernard, *Elliott Carter*, 108; and in Felix Meyer and Anne C. Shref-

fler, *Elliott Carter: A Centennial Portrait in Letters and Documents* (Suffolk: Boydell Press, 2008), 25.

9. Carter, "The Case of Mr. Ives," *Modern Music* 16, no. 3 (1939): 172, in Stone and Stone, *Writings*, 48; in Bernard, *Elliott Carter*, 87.

10. Carter, "Charles Ives Remembered," in Stone and Stone, *Writings*, 264; in Bernard, *Elliott Carter*, 103.

11. Carter, in Edwards, *Flawed Words*, 43.

12. Ibid., 42.

13. Ibid., 45.

14. Ibid.

15. Ibid., 46.

16. Carter, "Walter Piston," *Musical Quarterly* 32, no. 3 (1946): 357, in Stone and Stone, *Writings*, 124; in Bernard, *Elliott Carter*, 161.

17. Ibid., 358, 359.

18. Carter, in Edwards, *Flawed Words*, 46.

19. Quoted in Matthew Guerrieri, "The Composer in Cambridge: Carter Looks Back," *Boston Globe*, 5 December 2008.

20. Quoted in Alan Baker, *An Interview with Elliott Carter*, American Public Radio, July 2002, http://musicmavericks.publicradio.org/features/interview_carter.html, accessed 7 April 2009.

21. David Ewen, *American Composers Today* (New York: H. W. Wilson, 1949), 48; David Schiff, *The Music of Elliott Carter*, 1st ed. (London: Eulenburg, 1983), 18; 2nd ed. (Ithaca, N.Y.: Cornell University Press, 1998), 12; Meyer and Shreffler, *Centennial Portrait*, 28.

22. Meyer and Shreffler, *Centennial Portrait*, 28.

23. Carter, letter to the editor, *Journal of Music Theory* 7, no. 2 (1963): 270–73.

24. Quoted in Guerrieri, "The Composer in Cambridge."

25. Jonathan W. Bernard, "Elliott Carter and the Modern Meaning of Time," *Musical Quarterly* 79, no. 4 (1995): 649, 645–46.

26. Carter, in Edwards, *Flawed Words*, 47.

27. Ibid.

28. Ibid.

29. Carter, "The Recent Works of Goffredo Petrassi," 1960, unpublished, in Bernard, *Elliott Carter*, 187.

30. Victor Lowe, *Understanding Whitehead* (Baltimore, Md.: Johns Hopkins Press, 1962), 228, quoted in Bernard, "Modern Meaning," 649, emphasis in the original.

31. Lowe, *Understanding Whitehead*, 38, in Bernard, "Modern Meaning," 649–50.

32. Bernard, "Modern Meaning," 650.

33. Ibid.

34. Carter, in Edwards, *Flawed Words*, 47–48, 47.

35. Ibid., 48.

36. Elliott Forbes, "A History of Music at Harvard to 1972," 62, quoted in Meyer and Shreffler, *Centennial Portrait*, 28.

37. Schiff, *Music of Elliott Carter*, 2nd ed., 12.

38. "'Philoctetes': Enthusiastic Lowell House Audience Applauds Classical Club's Staging of Tragedy," n.d., quoted in Meyer and Shreffler, *Centennial Portrait*, 30.

39. Schiff, *Music of Elliott Carter*, 2nd ed., 12.

40. Carter, in Edwards, *Flawed Words*, 49–50.

41. For more on Boulanger's career, see Bruce A. Brown, "Leçon de musique avec Nadia Boulanger," *Music Educators Journal* 69, no. 1 (1982): 49–51; Jeanice Brooks, "Nadia Boulanger and the Salon of the Princesse de Polignac," *Journal of the American Musicological Society* 46, no. 3 (1993): 415–68; and Caroline Potter, "Nadia and Lili Boulanger: Sister Composers," *Musical Quarterly* 83, no. 4 (1999): 536–56.

42. Ives's strong admonition was reported by Carter in an interview with Meyer and Shreffler in January 2008; it is paraphrased in Meyer and Shreffler, *Centennial Portrait*, 32.

43. Schiff, *Music of Elliott Carter*, 2nd ed., 12.

44. Meyer and Shreffler, *Centennial Portrait*, 32.

45. Carter, "'Elle est la musique en personne': A Reminiscence of Nadia Boulanger" (ca. 1985–95), in Bernard, *Elliott Carter*, 218.

46. Schiff, *Music of Elliott Carter*, 1st ed., 16. Meyer and Shreffler write that during his father's lifetime, that is, until 1955, "Carter received a modest allowance of somewhat less than $500 per year, which although not nearly enough to live on, helped to supplement his income during his studies and early career" (*Centennial Portrait*, 24).

47. Schiff, *Music of Elliott Carter*, 1st ed., 16.

48. Carter, in Edwards, *Flawed Words*, 51.

49. Schiff, *Music of Elliott Carter*, 1st ed., 20, emphasis added.

50. Carter, "Elle est la musique," in Bernard, *Elliott Carter*, 290.

51. Carter, in Edwards, *Flawed Words*, 50.

52. Carter, "Elle est la musique," in Bernard, *Elliott Carter*, 283.

53. Carter, in Edwards, *Flawed Words*, 50.

54. Carter, "Elle est la musique," in Bernard, *Elliott Carter*, 292.

55. Ibid.

56. Ibid.

57. Schiff, *Music of Elliott Carter*, 1st ed., 20.

58. Meyer and Shreffler, *Centennial Portrait*, 47.

59. Carter to Walter Piston, quoted by Bernard in his introduction to *Elliott Carter*, vii. The letter exists only in a pencil draft; it is not dated, and Bernard notes that it was written "probably early in 1936."

60. Stone and Stone, introductory note to *Writings*, xi.

61. Claire R. Reis, *Composers in America: Biographical Sketches of Living Composers with a Record of Their Works, 1912–1937* (New York: Macmillan, 1938), 72.

62. John Martin, "Ballet Caravan in Seasonal Debut," *New York Times*, 25 May 1939.

63. Olga Naumoff (Koussevitzky's secretary) to Carter, 4 December 1939, reproduced in Meyer and Shreffler, *Centennial Portrait*, 44.

64. "'Pocahontas' Suite Wins Competition," *New York Times*, 4 June 1940.

65. Meyer and Shreffler, *Centennial Portrait*, 37.

66. Carter, "Music as a Liberal Art," *Modern Music* 22, no. 1 (1944): 12–16, reproduced in Stone and Stone, *Writings*, 102–6; in Bernard, *Elliott Carter*, 309–13.

67. Carter, in Edwards, *Flawed Words*, 57–58.

68. Carter, in an interview with Nicholas Wroe, *Guardian*, 6 December 2008, http://www.guardian.co.uk/music/2008/dec/06/elliott-carter-classical-music.

69. Carter to John Kirkpatrick, 1 April 1944, quoted in Meyer and Shreffler, *Centennial Portrait*, 51.

70. Meyer and Shreffler, *Centennial Portrait*, 63.

71. Carter, in Edwards, *Flawed Words*, 57–58.

72. Ibid., 58.

73. Goldman, "Music of Elliott Carter," 156.

74. Ned Rorem, "Messiaen and Carter on Their Birthdays," *Tempo*, n.s., no. 127 (1978): 23.

CHAPTER 2. *Three Seminal Works (1945–51)*

1. David Schiff, *The Music of Elliott Carter*, 1st ed. (London: Eulenberg, 1983), 76.

2. Jonathan W. Bernard, "The Evolution of Elliott Carter's Rhythmic Practice," *Perspectives of New Music* 26, no. 2 (1988): 165.

3. Michael Cherlin, "Crossing the Millennium with Elliott Carter," *Music Theory Spectrum* 23, no. 1 (2001): 103.

4. John Rockwell, "Elliott Carter: American Intellectual Composers & the 'Ideal Public,'" in *All American Music: Composition in the Late Twentieth Century* (New York: Alfred A. Knopf, 1983), 38, emphasis added.

5. Bernard, "Evolution."

6. Carter, in Allen Edwards, *Flawed Words and Stubborn Sounds: A Conversation with Elliott Carter* (New York: W. W. Norton, 1971), 59.

7. Jonathan W. Bernard, "Elliott Carter and the Modern Meaning of Time," *Musical Quarterly* 79, no. 4 (1995): 677. Bernard's paraphrase of Carter's words is based on an unpublished Carter essay titled "My Neoclassicism." Regrettably, "My Neoclassicism" is not included in *Elliott Carter: Collected Essays and Lectures, 1937–1995*, ed. Bernard (Rochester, N.Y.: University of Rochester Press, 1997).

8. Dwight Macdonald, "The Absent-Minded Professor," *Politics*, October 1946. Reprinted in Dwight Macdonald, *Discriminations: Essays and Afterthoughts* (New York: Da Capo Press, 1974), 371–72.

9. Martin Boykan, "Elliott Carter and the Postwar Composers," *Perspectives of New Music* 2, no. 2 (1964): 125, 128.

10. Carter, in Edwards, *Flawed Words*, 90, emphasis in the original.

11. Bernard, "Modern Meaning," 655–56. The quotation is from Edwards, *Flawed Words*, 101.

12. Carter, in Edwards, *Flawed Words*, 90.

13. Ibid., 90–91.

14. Ibid., 91. Along with Arabic, Indian, and Indonesian rhythmic practice, rhythm in the music of Africa's Watusi tribe at this time held special interest for Carter.

15. Ibid. Carter's comments in the Edwards book are presented as though they are thoughtful but nevertheless spontaneous responses to Edwards's questions. In this case, the comments come almost verbatim from the liner notes that Carter wrote in 1969 for a recording (Nonesuch H-71234) of his 1948 Piano Sonata and 1952 Sonata for Flute, Oboe, Cello, and Harpsichord. The liner notes are reproduced under the title "Sonata for Cello

and Piano (1948)/Sonata for Flue, Oboe, Cello, and Harpsichord (1952)" in *The Writings of Elliott Carter*, ed. Else Stone and Kurt Stone (Bloomington: Indiana University Press, 1977), 269–73; and under the title "Two Sonatas, 1948 and 1952" in Bernard, *Elliott Carter*, 228–31.

16. Edwards, *Flawed Words*, 91.

17. Richard Franko Goldman, "Current Chronicle," *Musical Quarterly* 37, no. 1 (1951): 87. The works that Goldman discusses are the 1948 Cello Sonata, the 1948 Woodwind Quintet, and the 1950 *Eight Etudes and a Fantasia* for woodwind quartet.

18. Edwards, *Flawed Words*, 91–92n.

19. Carter, in ibid., 91.

20. Carter, in ibid., 92, emphasis in the original.

21. Ibid., 92–93.

22. *Emblems* was written for the Harvard Glee Club in 1947 but not performed in its entirety, by the Colgate College Singers, until the summer of 1952.

23. The letter (from January 1946) in which Kirkpatrick reneges on his commitment to premiere the Piano Sonata is quoted in Meyer and Shreffler, *Centennial Portrait*, 73.

24. Virgil Thomson, "Fulfillment Experienced," *New York Herald Tribune*, 13 March 1948. The complete review is reproduced in Virgil Thomson, *Music Reviewed, 1940–1954* (New York: Vintage Books, 1967), 244–45.

25. C.H., "Aitken Introduces Work by Menotti—Pianist Includes Ives, Carter and Beethoven Compositions in Recital at Town Hall," *New York Times*, 13 March 1948.

26. Carter, "Analysis of the Piano Sonata," quoted in Meyer and Shreffler, *Centennial Portrait*, 77.

27. Ibid.

28. Carter, "Artistic Credo," quoted in ibid., 79.

29. Carter, "The Composer's Choices" (ca. 1960), in Stone and Stone, *Writings*, 195; in Bernard, *Elliott Carter*, 213.

30. Carter, "Artistic Credo."

31. Carter, in Charles Rosen, "An Interview with Elliott Carter," in *The Musical Languages of Elliott Carter* (Washington, D.C.: Library of Congress, 1984), 33–34.

32. Bernard, "Evolution," 170.

33. Schiff, *Music of Elliott Carter*, 1st ed., 132; Bernard, "Evolution," 170.

34. Carter, in Benjamin Boretz, "Conversation with Elliott Carter," *Perspectives of New Music* 8, no. 2 (1970): 18, emphasis added.

35. Ibid., 18–19.

36. Carter, in Edwards, *Flawed Words*, 35.

37. Carter, liner notes for the 1970 recording, by the Composers String Quartet, of his quartets nos. 1 and 2 (Nonesuch H-71249). The liner-note essay is reproduced in Stone and Stone, *Writings*, 274–79; in Bernard, *Elliott Carter*, 231–35.

38. The first commercial recording of Carter's music—featuring the Piano Sonata performed by Beveridge Webster and the Cello Sonata performed by cellist Bernard Greenhouse and pianist Anthony Makas—was released early in 1951 by the American Recording Society (ARS-2335); the monophonic recording was rereleased on the Desto label (D-419) in 1965.

39. Carter, in Edwards, *Flawed Words*, 35.

40. Carter, liner notes for Nonesuch H-71249, in Stone and Stone, *Writings*, 275; in Bernard, *Elliott Carter*, 23. The comment is presented within quotation marks and attributed to Joseph Wood Krutch, a naturalist who was Carter's neighbor during the Tucson sojourn.

41. Carter, in Edwards, *Flawed Words*, 35.

42. Carter, "Shop Talk by an American Composer," *Musical Quarterly* 46, no. 2 (1960): 193, in Stone and Stone, *Writings*, 203–4; in Bernard, *Elliott Carter*, 217–18.

43. Ibid., emphasis added; Bernard, "Evolution," 176.

44. An excerpt from the score, annotated to show the different rates of flow, appears in Bernard, "Evolution," 175. Without annotations, the same excerpt appears in Schiff, *Music of Elliott Carter*, 2nd ed., 58.

45. The notes are identified here and throughout this book only by their pitch-class names. For the specific notation, see measures 1–16 of the Cello Sonata as reproduced in Bernard, "Evolution," 172.

46. Schiff, *Music of Elliott Carter*, 2nd ed., 137.

47. This now-standard method of labeling pitch-class sets, in which the pitches are first compressed into their smallest possible range and then identified according to their distance (measured in half steps) from the pitch that represents the outer extreme of the smallest interval, was first proposed by Allen Forte in his *The Structure of Atonal Music* (New Haven, Conn.: Yale University Press, 1973), 1–2. A clear explanation of the labeling system is offered in Joseph Nathan Straus, *Introduction to Post-Tonal Theory* (Englewood Cliffs, N.J.: Prentice-Hall, 1990).

48. Carter, "Shop Talk," 194–95, emphasis added, in Stone and Stone, *Writings*, 305; in Bernard, *Elliott Carter*, 219.

49. Carter, liner notes for Nonesuch H-71249, in Stone and Stone, *Writings*, 276–77; in Bernard, *Elliott Carter*, 233.

50. Richard Franko Goldman, "The Music of Elliott Carter," *Musical Quarterly* 63, no. 2 (1957): 162.

51. William E. Brandt, "The Music of Elliott Carter: Simultaneity and Complexity," *Music Educators Journal* 60, no. 9 (1974): 28.

52. Carter, liner notes for Nonesuch H-71249, in Stone and Stone, *Writings*, 277; in Bernard, *Elliott Carter*, 233.

53. Schiff, *Music of Elliott Carter*, 1st ed., 152. In the second edition of *The Music of Elliott Carter* (Ithaca, N.Y.: Cornell University Press, 1998), Schiff expresses a more reserved opinion, writing only that "the wealth of relationships and dreamlike continuity of the quartet were meant to translate the formal devices of Eliot, Joyce, Proust or Eisenstein into musical terms" (55).

54. Carter, "Shop Talk," 191, in Stone and Stone, *Writings*, 202; in Bernard, *Elliott Carter*, 216.

55. Carter, "Music and the Time Screen," in *Current Thought in Musicology*, ed. John W. Grubbs (Austin: University of Texas Press, 1976), 88, in Stone and Stone, *Writings*, 363–64; in Bernard, *Elliott Carter*, 280.

56. Wilfrid Mellers, *Music in a New Found Land: Themes and Developments in the History of American Music* (New York: Alfred A. Knopf, 1964), 106–7.

57. Paul Griffiths, *Modern Music and After: Directions since 1945* (Oxford: Oxford University Press, 1995), 53, 54.

58. Carter, "Music and the Time Screen," in Stone and Stone, *Writings*, 364; in Bernard, *Elliott Carter*, 280.

CHAPTER 3. *Maturity (1950–80)*

1. The commission was for a sonata for two pianos. Carter began work on the piece late in 1953 and returned to it two years later, but he never finished it.

2. Ostensibly an international organization, the Paris-based Congress for Cultural Freedom was secretly funded by the U.S. Central Intelligence Agency. For more on the relationship between the CIA and modernist culture, see Frances Stonor Saunders, *Who Paid the Piper?: The CIA and the Cultural Cold War* (London: Granta Books, 1999); and Mark Carroll, *Music and Ideology in Cold War Europe* (Cambridge: Cambridge University Press, 2003).

3. David Schiff, *The Music of Elliott Carter*, 1st ed. (London: Eulenburg, 1983), 152; 2nd ed. (Ithaca, N.Y.: Cornell University Press, 1998), 55, 53.

4. Reginald Smith Brindle, "Notes from Abroad," *Musical Times* 95, no. 1,336 (1954): 328; William Glock, "Music Festival in Rome," *Encounters* 2, no. 6 (1954): 63; Harold C. Schonberg, "Carter Composition in World Premiere," *New York Times*, 27 February 1953.

5. Martin Boykan, "Elliott Carter and the Postwar Composers," *Perspectives of New Music* 2, no. 2 (1964): 125, emphasis added.

6. Schiff, *Music of Elliott Carter*, 2nd ed., 24, 27. The single exception is the 1978 *Birthday Fanfare* for three trumpets, vibraphone, and glockenspiel that Carter wrote to help celebrate the seventieth birthday of British critic and broadcast executive William Glock.

7. Ibid., 25.

8. Carter, "Reminiscence of Italy," in *Elliott Carter: Collected Essays and Lectures, 1937–1995*, ed. Jonathan W. Bernard (Rochester, N.Y.: University of Rochester Press, 1997), 294.

9. The summer school was first based at Bryanston in Dorset. It relocated to the Dartington Hall estate in Devon in 1953.

10. Titled "The Rhythmic Basis of American Music," Carter's article appeared in the *Score* in June 1955. It is reproduced in *The Writings of Elliott Carter*, ed. Else Stone and Kurt Stone (Bloomington: Indiana University Press, 1977), 160–66, and in Bernard, *Elliott Carter*, 57–62.

11. For accounts of Carter's teaching authored by his former students, see Alvin Curran, "e poi . . . ," in *Elliott Carter: A Centennial Celebration*, ed. Marc Ponthus and Susan Tang (Hillsdale, N.Y.: Pendragon Press, 2008), 41–46; and David Schiff, review of *Elliott Carter: Harmony Book*, *Tempo* 57 (2003): 53–55.

12. The commission came in 1956, from the Stanley Quartet based at the University of Michigan. The Stanley Quartet found the piece too difficult to play, and thus the premiere was granted to the Juilliard Quartet.

13. Initiated in 1947 by Harvard student Clemens Heller and supported through private funding, the Salzburg Seminars in American Studies program was housed in the Schloss

Leopoldskron, an eighteenth-century palace that was once the home of the city's archbishop. In the 1965 film *The Sound of Music*, the Schloss Leopoldskron played the role of the Trapp family residence.

14. Carter to Petrassi, 8 January 1959, paraphrased by Felix Meyer and Anne C. Shreffler, *Elliott Carter: A Centennial Portrait in Letters and Documents* (Suffolk: Boydell Press, 2008), 152–53.

15. Carter to Peter Yates, 8 June 1959, quoted in ibid., 155.

16. Along with the above-mentioned June 1955 article ("The Rhythmic Basis of American Music") for the *Score*, these include "La Musique aux Etats-Unis" (published in the Belgian journal *Synthèses* in May 1954); a speech titled "The Agony of Modern Music in America" (delivered at the 1955 ISCM festival in Baden-Baden); a 1958 overview of American music titled "A Further Step" (originally published in Spanish in the Argentine journal *Buenos Aires Musical* in December 1959, then published in English translation as a chapter of *The American Composer Speaks: 1770–1965*, ed. Gilbert Chase [Baton Rouge: Louisiana State University Press, 1966]); the 1960 essay "Shop Talk by an American Composer" (*Musical Quarterly* 46, no. 2); and a 1961 radio address originally titled "The European Roots of American Musical Culture" that was published in truncated form in 1962 as "The Milieu of the American Composer" (*Perspectives of New Music* 1, no. 1).

17. Various letters in which Carter explains his reasons for declining the invitations—his refusal, in short, to have either himself or his music used for the purposes of political propaganda—are reproduced in Meyer and Shreffler, *Centennial Portrait*, 160–61.

18. Carter, "Reminiscence of Italy," in Bernard, *Elliott Carter*, 294.

19. Schiff, *Music of Elliott Carter*, 2nd ed., 25. Schiff does not cite a source for this comment; presumably Carter made the comment in a private conservation.

20. Ibid., 53.

21. Carter, "The Time Dimension in Music," *Music Journal* 23, no. 8 (1965): 29, in Stone and Stone, *Writings*, 243; in Bernard, *Elliott Carter*, 224–25. Carter's essay was based on a lecture delivered in the summer of 1965 at both Bowdoin College and the University of Texas at Austin.

22. Schiff, *Music of Elliott Carter*, 1st ed., 193.

23. Jonathan W. Bernard, "An Interview with Elliott Carter," *Perspectives of New Music* 28, no. 2 (1990): 196.

24. Ibid., 197, emphasis in the original. Clearly influenced by Messiaen (1908–92), in 1951 both Boulez (1925–) and Stockhausen (1928–2007) experimented with so-called total serialism in *Structures* for two pianos and *Kreuzspiel* for piano, winds, and percussion, respectively.

25. Ibid., emphasis added.

26. Carter, "Music and the Time Screen," in *Current Thought in Musicology*, ed. John W. Grubbs (Austin: University of Texas Press, 1976), 70, in Stone and Stone, *Writings*, 351; in Bernard, *Elliott Carter*, 270. Mann's novel was published in 1924 and first appeared in English translation in 1927.

27. Ibid.

28. Whitehead's often quoted statement was first articulated in his 1919 "The Concept of Nature" lecture at Trinity College in Cambridge, England.

29. The text of the lecture is reproduced in Meyer and Shreffler, *Centennial Portrait*, 130–37.

30. See notes 17 and 22. "The Time Dimension in Music" is reproduced in Stone and Stone, *Writings*, 243–47; in Bernard, *Elliott Carter*, 224–28. "Music and the Time Screen" is reproduced in Stone and Stone, *Writings*, 343–65; in Bernard, *Elliott Carter*, 262–80.

31. Carter's 1976 "Time Lecture" (as revised in 1994) is reproduced only in Bernard, *Elliott Carter*, 313–18.

32. Jonathan W. Bernard, "Elliott Carter and the Modern Meaning of Time," *Musical Quarterly* 79, no. 4 (1995): 645–46. The Koechlin article first appeared in *Revue Musicale* 7, no. 3 (1926): 45–62; the Suvchinsky article appeared in *Revue Musicale* 20 (May–June 1939): 310–20; the 1949 Brelet volumes were published in Paris by Presses Universitaires de France.

33. Meyer and Shreffler, *Centennial Portrait*, 129.

34. Carter, "Sound and Silence in Time," in ibid., 135.

35. Ibid., 136–37.

36. Ibid., 136.

37. Ibid., 136.

38. Carter, "Music and the Time Screen," in Stone and Stone, *Writings*, 344; in Bernard, *Elliott Carter*, 263.

39. Carter, "Time Lecture," in Bernard, *Elliott Carter*, 314–15.

40. Carter, "Music and the Time Screen," in Stone and Stone, *Writings*, 344–49, 363; in Bernard, *Elliott Carter*, 263–66, 278.

41. Ibid., in Stone and Stone, *Writings*, 345; in Bernard, *Elliott Carter*, 263.

42. Susanne K. Langer, *Feeling and Form* (New York: Charles Scribner's Sons, 1953), 114, quoted in Carter, "Music and the Time Screen," in Stone and Stone, *Writings*, 345; in Bernard, *Elliott Carter*, 263.

43. Langer, *Feeling and Form*, 112–13, quoted in Carter, "Music and the Time Screen," in Stone and Stone, *Writings*, 346; in Bernard, *Elliott Carter*, 264–65, emphasis in the original in Langer; ellipses original in Carter.

In the sections of the passage that Carter skips over, Langer calls italicized attention to two other words whose underlying concepts relate importantly to Carter's thinking. She writes: "The phenomena that fill time are *tensions*—physical, emotional, or intellectual" and "Some [tensions] drive and some drag, but for perception they give *quality* rather than form to the passage of time, which unfolds in the pattern of the dominant and distinct strains whereby we are measuring it" (*Feeling and Form*, 112, 113).

44. Carter, "The Time Dimension in Music," in Stone and Stone, *Writings*, 243; in Bernard, *Elliott Carter*, 225.

45. Carter, "Time Lecture," in Bernard, *Elliott Carter*, 318, emphasis added.

46. Carter, in Benjamin Boretz, "Conversation with Elliott Carter," *Perspectives of New Music* 8, no. 2 (1970): 13.

47. Carter, "Music and the Time Screen," in Stone and Stone, *Writings*, 353; in Bernard, *Elliott Carter*, 270.

48. Ibid., in Stone and Stone, *Writings*, 353; in Bernard, *Elliott Carter*, 271.

49. Carter, in Bernard, "Interview," 203.

50. Carter, "Music and the Time Screen," in Stone and Stone, *Writings*, 355; in Bernard, *Elliott Carter*, 273.

51. Carter, "The Time Dimension in Music," in Stone and Stone, *Writings*, 246; in Bernard, *Elliott Carter*, 227.

52. Schiff, *Music of Elliott Carter*, 1st ed., 211, 2nd ed., 242.

53. Carter, "The Time Dimension in Music," in Stone and Stone, *Writings*, 247; in Bernard, *Elliott Carter*, 227–28.

54. Carter, in Allen Edwards, *Flawed Words and Stubborn Sounds: A Conversation with Elliott Carter* (New York: W. W. Norton, 1971), 104.

55. Jonathan W. Bernard, "The Evolution of Elliott Carter's Rhythmic Practice," *Perspectives of New Music* 26, no. 2 (1988): 192, emphasis added.

56. Carter, "Music and the Time Screen," in Stone and Stone, *Writings*, 357; in Bernard, *Elliott Carter*, 277.

57. Carter, "La musique sérielle aujourd'hui," in Bernard, *Elliott Carter*, 18. Carter's brief article was published in *Preuves* 177 (November 1965): 32–33. The text in the Bernard anthology is Carter's original English version. Along with Robbe-Grillet, the authors Carter mentions are James Joyce, Marcel Proust, Michel Butor, and William S. Burroughs.

There is no doubt that Carter eventually was familiar with *Last Year at Marienbad*, for he mentions it—along with several dozen other films—in a list of cinematic favorites he prepared in 1992 in anticipation of a Rotterdam festival in his honor. Carter's letter to Dutch filmmaker Frank Scheffer is reproduced in Meyer and Sheffler, *Centennial Portrait*, 290–91.

58. Alain Robbe-Grillet, "Alain Robbe-Grillet vous parle de *L'Année dernière à Marienbad*," trans. Richard Howard, emphasis in the original. Robbe-Grillet's article first appeared in the Paris magazine *Réalités* in May 1961; the translation by Howard first appeared as the introduction to the English-language version of the screenplay published by Grove Press (London) in 1962. The quoted excerpt is from p. 23 of the translated article as reprinted in the booklet accompanying the 2009 Criterion Collection DVD edition of *Last Year at Marienbad* (CC1815D).

59. Ibid., 30.

60. Ibid., 33.

61. Carter, in Edwards, *Flawed Words*, 101; and Carter, "Music and the Time Screen," in Stone and Stone, *Writings*, 355–56; in Bernard, *Elliott Carter*, 274.

62. Carter, liner note for the 1970 recording, by the Composers Quartet, of his string quartets nos. 1 and 2 (Nonesuch H-71249), in Stone and Stone, *Writings*, 278; in Bernard, *Elliott Carter*, 234.

63. Carter, "Music and the Time Screen," in Stone and Stone, *Writings*, 355–56; in Bernard, *Elliott Carter*, 273.

64. Ibid., emphasis added.

65. Bernard, "Modern Meaning," 673.

66. Meyer and Shreffler, *Centennial Portrait*, 205.

67. Andrew Porter, "Mutual Ordering," *New Yorker*, 3 February 1974, in *A Musical Season: A Critic from Abroad in America* (New York: Viking Press, 1974), 140.

68. Andrew Porter, "Famous Orpheus," *New Yorker*, 8 January 1979, in *Music of Three More Seasons: 1977–1980* (New York: Alfred A. Knopf, 1981), 281.

69. Virgil Thomson, *American Music since 1910* (New York: Holt, Rinehart and Winston, 1971), 37–38, 130.

70. Irving Kolodin, *In Quest of Music: A Journey in Time* (New York: Doubleday, 1980), 309–10.

71. Ned Rorem, "Setting the Tone," *Christopher Street* magazine, 1980, in *Setting the Tone: Essays and a Diary* (New York: Coward-McCann, 1983), 93.

72. Rorem, "Our Music Now," *New Republic*, 1974, in *Settling the Score: Essays on Music* (New York: Harcourt Brace Jovanovich, 1988), 281–82, emphasis in the original.

73. Leonard B. Meyer, "Some Remarks on Value and Greatness in Music," *Journal of Aesthetics and Art Criticism* 17, no. 4 (1959): 500. Meyer's essay is reproduced as chapter 2 of his *Music, the Arts, and Ideas: Patterns and Predictions in Twentieth-Century Culture* (Chicago: University of Chicago Press, 1967).

74. Bennett Reimer, "Leonard Meyer's Theory of Value and Greatness in Music," *Journal of Research in Music Education* 10, no. 2 (1962): 98.

75. Alfred Einstein, *Greatness in Music*, trans. César Saerchinger (New York: Oxford University Press, 1942), 129, 139, 163.

CHAPTER 4. *New Directions (1980–2010)*

1. The Siemens Prize granted Carter in 1981 carried a cash award of 150,000 Swiss francs, an amount equivalent today to approximately $135,000; in marked contrast, the Nobel Prize typically carries a cash award equivalent to approximately $1 million. The Nobel Prize was established in 1895 by the Swedish chemist Alfred Nobel (inventor of, among other things, dynamite); the Siemens Prize was established in 1972 by Ernst von Siemens, the grandson and heir of Werner von Siemens, the nineteenth-century inventor of a great many electrical devices. Before Carter, the Siemens Prize had been awarded only to composers Benjamin Britten and Olivier Messiaen (1973 and 1975, respectively), cellist Mstislav Rostropovich (1976), conductor Herbert von Karajan (1977), pianist Rudolf Serkin (1978), composer/conductor Pierre Boulez (1979), and baritone Dietrich Fischer-Dieskau (1980).

2. Award certificate for the 1981 Ernst von Siemens Prize, in Felix Meyer and Anne C. Shreffler, *Elliott Carter: A Centennial Portrait in Letters and Documents* (Suffolk: Boydell Press, 2008), 241.

3. Carter, acceptance speech for the Ernst von Siemens Prize, 8 April 1981, in ibid., 243.

4. David Schiff, *The Music of Elliott Carter*, 2nd ed. (Ithaca, N.Y.: Cornell University Press, 1998), 199.

5. Ibid., 28.

6. Charles Wuorinen, review of the first edition of David Schiff, *The Music of Elliott Carter*, *Musical Quarterly* 69, no. 4 (1983): 606.

7. Robert P. Morgan, review of the first edition of David Schiff, *The Music of Elliott Carter*, *Journal of Musicology* 2, no. 3 (1983): 340.

8. Arnold Whittall, review of the first edition of David Schiff, *The Music of Elliott Carter*, *Music & Letters* 65, no. 3 (1984): 276.

9. David Harvey, review of the first edition of David Schiff, *The Music of Elliott Carter*, *Musical Times* 124, no. 1,685 (1983): 426.

10. Robert D. Morris, review of the first edition of David Schiff, *The Music of Elliott Carter, Journal of the American Musicological Society* 38, no. 1 (1985): 184–85.

11. Ibid., 183; Wuorinen, review, 606, emphasis added.

12. Edward Said, *On Late Style: Music and Literature against the Grain* (New York: Vintage Books, 2006), 7, emphasis and final ellipsis in the original.

13. Ibid., 4.

14. Schiff, *The Music of Elliott Carter*, 2nd ed., 29.

15. David Schiff, "Elliott Carter's Harvest Home," *Tempo* 167 (December 1988): 2.

16. Italo Calvino, *Six Memos for the Next Millennium*, trans. Patrick Creagh (Cambridge, Mass.: Harvard University Press, 1988), 1. Originally published as *Lezioni americane: Sei proposte per il prossimo millennio* (Milan: Garzanti, 1988).

17. Carter, in Allen Edwards, *Flawed Words and Stubborn Sounds: A Conversation with Elliott Carter* (New York: W. W. Norton, 1971), 101.

18. Calvino, *Six Memos*, 45.

19. Ibid., 12.

20. Ibid., 10–17.

21. Schiff, *The Music of Elliott Carter*, 2nd ed., 120.

22. Arnold Whittall, "Summer's Long Shadows," *Musical Times* 138, no. 1,850 (1997): 14.

23. David Schiff, "Carter's New Classicism," *College Music Symposium* 29 (1989): 120.

24. Schiff, *The Music of Elliott Carter*, 2nd ed., 29–30.

25. Ibid., 30.

26. Carter, program note for the Quintet for Piano and Winds, quoted in Whittall, "Summer's Long Shadows," 16.

27. Ibid., 18.

28. Ibid., 21.

29. Schiff, *The Music of Elliott Carter*, 2nd ed., 30.

30. Whittall, "Summer's Long Shadows," 21.

31. Said, *On Late Style*, 6–7.

32. Jonathan W. Bernard, "An Introduction to the Music of Carter," Boosey & Hawkes Web site, 1994, http://www.boosey.com/pages/cr/composer/composer_main.asp?composerid=2790&ttype=INTRODUCTION&title=IN%20Focus.

33. Jonathan W. Bernard, "The Evolution of Elliott Carter's Rhythmic Practice," *Perspectives of New Music* 26, no. 2 (1988): 166.

34. Morgan, review, 340.

35. Carter, "Shop Talk by an American Composer," *Musical Quarterly* 46, no. 2 (1960): 200, in *The Writings of Elliott Carter*, ed. Else Stone and Kurt Stone (Bloomington: Indiana University Press, 1977), 208; and in *Elliott Carter: Collected Essays and Lectures, 1937–1995*, ed. Jonathan W. Bernard (Rochester, N.Y.: University of Rochester Press, 1997), 221.

36. Samuel Lipman, "Doing New Music, Doing American Music," *New Criterion* 6, no. 3 (1987): 11.

37. Richard Taruskin, "The Poietic Fallacy," *Musical Times* 145, no. 1,886 (2004): 17.

38. David Schiff, liner notes for *Elliott Carter: Eight Compositions (1948–1993)* (Bridge Records BCD 9044), quoted by David Nicholls in a review of the recording in *American Music* 20, no. 2 (2002): 236.

39. Carter, in Nicholas Wroe, "A Life in Music: Elliott Carter," *Guardian*, 6 September 2008.

40. Carter, in Sue Knussen, "Elliott Carter in Interview," *Tempo*, n.s., no. 197 (1996): 5.

41. Bernard, "Introduction."

42. Edwards, *Flawed Words*, 60; Jonathan W. Bernard, "Elliott Carter and the Modern Meaning of Time," *Musical Quarterly* 79, no. 4 (1995): 677. Bernard here paraphrases Carter's as yet unpublished essay "My Neoclassicism."

43. Schiff, "Carter's New Classicism," 115.

44. Schiff draws especially from Barthes' *S/Z*, first published in 1970 (Paris: Seuil) and then, in an English translation by Richard Miller, in 1974 (New York: Hill and Wang).

45. Schiff, "Carter's New Classicism," 115.

46. Jonathan Kramer, "Postmodern Concepts of Musical Time," *Indiana Theory Review* 17, no. 2 (1996): 21–22.

47. Jonathan Kramer, "The Nature and Origins of Musical Postmodernism," *Current Musicology* 66 (1999): 7; Lawrence Kramer, *Classical Music and Postmodern Knowledge* (Berkeley: University of California Press, 1995), 5; Richard Taruskin, "After Everything," in *The Oxford History of Western Music* (Oxford: Oxford University Press, 2005), 5:412.

48. Schiff, "Carter's New Classicism," 115.

49. Antony Bye, "Carter's 'Classic' Modernism," *Tempo*, n.s., no. 189 (1994): 2.

50. Ibid., 3.

51. Arnold Whittall, review of Carter's Oboe Concerto (full score), *Music & Letters* 73, no. 2 (1992): 40.

52. Whittall, "Summer's Long Shadows," 14.

53. Ibid., 21.

54. Ronald Caltabiano, "Elliott Carter: Toward the Tenth Decade," *Tempo*, n.s., no. 207 (1998): 2.

55. *Symphonia*'s first movement, *Partita*, was commissioned by the Chicago Symphony Orchestra and premiered by that ensemble, under the direction of Daniel Barenboim, in Chicago's Orchestra Hall on 17 February 1994. The second movement, *Adagio tenebroso*, was commissioned by the BBC and premiered by the BBC Symphony Orchestra, under the direction of Andrew Davis, at London's Royal Albert Hall on 13 September 1995. The third movement, *Allegro scorrevole*, was originally commissioned by Zubin Mehta and the New York Philharmonic to celebrate the orchestra's sesquicentennial; after the Philharmonic's newly appointed music director, Kurt Masur, refused to commit to a performance until he had examined the score, the commission was taken up by the Cleveland Orchestra; *Allegro scorrevole* was given its premiere by the Cleveland Orchestra, under the direction of Christoph von Dohnányi, in Cleveland's Severance Hall on 22 May 1997. The three movements were given their first combined performance by the BBC Symphony Orchestra, under the direction of Oliver Knussen, who had originated the idea for *Symphonia*, in Manchester's Bridgewater Hall on 25 April 1998.

56. *Three Occasions* comprises the 1986 *A Celebration of Some 100 x 150 Notes*, the 1988 *Remembrance*, and the *Anniversary;* it has a total duration of just sixteen minutes. Such works as the 1955 Variations for Orchestra, the 1969 Concerto for Orchestra, and the 1976 A

Symphony of Three Orchestras have, on average, durations of between twenty and twenty-five minutes.

57. David Schiff, "Carter as Symphonist: Redefining Boundaries," *Musical Times* 139, no. 1,865 (1998): 13.

58. Whittall, "Summer's Long Shadows," 16; Schiff, "Carter as Symphonist," 13; Caltabiano, "Elliott Carter," 7.

59. Schiff, "Carter as Symphonist," 13.

60. Ibid.

61. Stephen Guy-Bray, "Pulchrum Spargitur Hic Chaos: Crashaw's Meta-Commentary," *Journal for Early Modern Cultural Studies* 9, no. 1 (2009): 157, 158. The quoted passage is from p. 13 of Schiff's "Carter as Symphonist."

62. Carter, in Andrew Ford, *Composer to Composer: Conversations about Contemporary Music* (London: Quartet Books, 1993), 19; Carter, spoken in Frank Scheffer, *Elliott Carter: A Labyrinth of Time* (Juxtapositions DVD9DS17, 2004), 14:43–15:16.

63. Schiff, "Carter as Symphonist," 13.

64. Meyer and Shreffler, *Centennial Portrait*, 309. The quoted review is Kyle Gann, "What Next?: Place Opera on Life's To-Do List," *New York Times*, 7 March 2000.

65. David Schiff, "Keeping Up with Carter," *Tempo*, n.s., no. 214 (2000): 3.

66. The *Elegy* was originally written in 1939 for cello and piano. Carter arranged the piece for string quartet in 1946, for string orchestra in 1952, and for viola and piano in 1961. The 2007 revisions are for both string quartet and cello-piano duo.

67. Meyer and Shreffler, *Centennial Portrait*, 312, 314.

68. Montale lived from 1896 to 1981; the poem "Tempo e tempi" is from his 1971 *Satura*. The translation is my own.

69. *More's Utopia* and *Fons juventatis* were combined in 2005 with *Micomicón* to form a three-movement work titled *Three Illusions*.

70. John Link, "Elliott Carter's 'Late Music'?" *Tempo* 62, no. 26 (2008): 7.

71. Ibid., 5.

Epilogue

1. H. Wiley Hitchcock, review of David Schiff, *The Music of Elliott Carter*, in *American Music* 6, no. 4 (1988): 468.

2. Leon Botstein, "Elliott Carter: An Appreciation," *Musical Quarterly* 91, nos. 3–4 (2008): 151; John F. Link, "Elliott Carter's 'Late Music'?" *Tempo* 62, no. 246 (2008): 10.

3. Arnold Whittall, "'A Play of Forces'? Elliott Carter's Opera in Context," *Musical Times* 149, no. 1,905 (2008): 3, 5.

4. Richard Taruskin, *The Oxford History of Western Music* (New York: Oxford University Press, 2005), 5:304.

5. Ibid., 5:265. The Rosen quotation—"it is important for a radically new work to be understood only little by little and too late [because] that is the only tangible proof we have of its revolutionary character"—comes originally from "One Easy Piece," *New York Review of Books*, 22 February 1973; the article, which deals primarily with Carter's Double

Concerto, is reprinted in *Critical Entertainments: Music Old and New* (Cambridge, Mass.: Harvard University Press, 2000).

6. Taruskin, *Oxford History*, 5:305.

7. For the sake of attacking Carter, Taruskin has quoted Rosen not just in the 2005 *Oxford History of Western Music* but also in "On Letting the Music Speak for Itself: Some Reflections of Musicology and Performance," *Journal of Musicology* 1, no. 3 (1982): 338–39; "The Poietic Fallacy," *Musical Times* 145, no. 1,886 (2004): 734; "The Musical Mystique: Defending Classical Music against Its Devotees," *New Republic*, 22 October 2007, 34–45; and "Afterword: *Nicht blutbefleckt?*" *Journal of Musicology* 26, no. 2 (2009): 274–84.

8. Charles Rosen, "Happy Birthday, Elliott Carter!" *New York Review of Books*, 12 March 2009, 31.

9. Charles Rosen, spoken in Frank Scheffer, *Elliott Carter: A Labyrinth of Time* (Juxtapositions DVD9DS17, 2004), 41:29–41:53.

10. Carter, in Benjamin Boretz, "Conversation with Elliott Carter," *Perspectives of New Music* 8, no. 2 (1970): 11–12, 14.

INDEX

JAMES WIERZBICKI teaches musicology at the University of Sydney, Australia, and is the author of *Film Music: A History* and *Louis and Bebe Barron's* Forbidden Planet*: A Film Score Guide*.

AMERICAN *Composers*

Lou Harrison
Leta E. Miller and Fredric Lieberman

John Cage
David Nicholls

Dudley Buck
N. Lee Orr

William Grant Smith
Catherine Parsons Smith

Rudolf Friml
William Everett

Elliott Carter
James Wierzbicki

The University of Illinois Press
is a founding member of the
Association of American University Presses.

Composed in 9.5/13 Janson Text
with Meta display
by Jim Proefrock
at the University of Illinois Press

Manufactured by Thomson-Shore, Inc.
University of Illinois Press
1325 South Oak Street
Champaign, IL 61820-6903
www.press.uillinois.edu